FW 8/16

DATE DUE FOR RETURN

- 2 SEP 2016

D1579688

Childwall Library

Renewals
www.liverpool.gov.uk/libraries
0151 233 3000

The Warriors and Wordsmiths of Freedom

The Birth and Growth of Democracy

LINDA MacDONALD-LEWIS

Luath Press Limited
EDINBURGH
www.luath.co.uk

First published 2009

ISBN: 978-1-906307-27-1

The author's right to be identified as author of this book
under the Copyright, Designs and Patents Act 1988
has been asserted.

The paper used in this book is neutral sized and recyclable.
It is made from elemental chlorine free pulps sourced from
renewable forests.

Printed and bound by
CPI Bookmarque, Croydon

Typeset in 10 point Sabon
by 3btype.com

Contents

Acknowledgements

Archie and Donna MacDonald (my parents), for setting my foot firmly on life's path and showing me the importance of honour, education, respect and love.

Lin and John Anderson, for their lasting friendship, undying support and inspiration. You've helped bring magic into my life.

Dr Elspeth King (at the Smith in Stirling), for her dedication and energy in keeping the history of Scotland alive and available to those who wish to listen and learn. You are my hero.

David R. Ross, for sharing his stories and his 'passion for Scotland' with the world at large. I'm proud to know you.

Gavin MacDougall (Luath Press, Edinburgh), for our ongoing relationship with books, poetry and music. Thanks for everything. You're a literary giant in my eyes.

Tim West, knowing you has been a complete pleasure. Who would have thought we'd be working together like this. Thanks for all your hard work and patience.

Leila Cruickshank, your keen eye, knowledge and endearing character has been the 'light on the pathway' for me. A heartfelt thanks to you and all the staff at Luath.

Thank you all for putting up with the likes of me for so long... or should I say, for so far!

This book is dedicated to

Freedom
and those
Warriors and Wordsmiths
who made it possible.

Now, Good King Robert the Bruce has delivered us up from these unbelievable evils, and has set free his people... And we will defend him with our own lives and our consent, as our chosen king...

But, if he should ever side against us and aid our enemies, we will bring him down from his position as king and cast him out as a subverter to our rights and the rights of our nation, and choose another to be our king to defend our freedoms.

DECLARATION OF ARBROATH, SCOTLAND 1320

[That] Governments are instituted among Men, deriving their just powers from the Consent of the Governed, that whenever any Form of Government becomes destructive of these ends, it is the Right of the People to alter or abolish it...

DECLARATION OF INDEPENDENCE,
UNITED STATES OF AMERICA 1776

For so long as a hundred of us remain alive,
we will never submit ourselves to English dominion.
We fight not for glory nor riches nor honours;
but only and alone we fight for freedom,
which no good man gives up,
but with his life.

DECLARATION OF ARBROATH, SCOTLAND 1320

If all else fails, I will retreat up the valley of Virginia, plant my flag on the Blue Ridge, rally around the Scotch–Irish of that region and make my last stand for liberty amongst a people who will never submit to British tyranny whilst there is a man left to draw a trigger...

GEORGE WASHINGTON AT VALLEY FORGE, WINTER 1777–78

Introduction

SCOTLAND! SO MANY things are said about her and still so little is truly understood.

Scotland, like many ancient cultures, means different things to different people:

She's mythological to those that study her...

She's historical to those that write about her...

She's romantic to those that yearn for her...

And she's mostly unseen by those that presently live between her shores.

The race of people known as the Scots have had a vast influence worldwide on inventions, music, sports, dress, and arts, and much has been written to reflect this. But beneath the surface of these material things lie the basic tenets, the cultural beliefs, the way of life, and the subtle social interactions that have ultimately led to the rest.

To understand the way of life in America, Americans should look to Scotland. It was in Scotland where the ideals of the people's democratic right to choose those who will lead them, or remove those from power if necessary, got its start.

The Declaration of Arbroath is believed to have been penned by Bernard de Linton, and opened the path for the later Wordsmiths who wrote about the rights of man, like George Buchanan, John Locke and Thomas Paine.

For those in Scotland to understand how these ideals, born in their own backyard, came to full fruition, they should study America. No other country in the world has embraced those doctrines more fully. The struggle for Independence in the formation of America holds many insights to the Independence issues being debated in Scotland today.

This book will explore a pathway of the belief held by the Scots, about the 'basic rights' that man is endowed with at birth. This belief, held by Celts as a 'free race', is woven into the fabric of life for the tribes that sprang from Scotland's ancient culture. Travelling through history, we'll see just how much influence this basic belief has had on great events in the past, and how much it has even now, on our modern world.

I suppose for me, seeing these differences started when I was young, with my Highland Scot father, Archie. Our very approach to life was not the same as that of our neighbours, who were Swedish, or German, or of other national birth or descent. Whenever we would question, 'Why do we do things this way, when the neighbours do that...', he'd say, 'Because you're a MacDonald! And don't you ever forget it!' When young, I had no idea that his pride in who he was extended further than just our name. It had to do with a national identity, a way of thinking and living, that was distinct: he was a Scot!

My parents always said that I was a wee bit different. That I never accepted what I was told without further investigation. At the age of five, I tried to find the eyes in the back of my mother's head, which she had boldly stated she possessed. This quirk in my personality, the influence of my parents, my fascination with learning, and a public library within walking distance, all helped begin my lifelong study of the Celtic realm at a very tender age. The never-ending reading on this subject is the one thing in my life that has been constant.

I never realised how much knowledge I had accumulated until I opened a Celtic shop in the 1990s and started fielding questions the public had about their heritage, and the history, mythology and folklore of Scotland and Ireland. Soon I came to understand how little people know about Scotland's past. But given a chance to learn, they are like sponges. People would hang out in the shop for hours on end to listen to the stories.

I was definitely in my element.

When I was asked by Gavin MacDougall of Luath Press to write a book about Scotland, I saw a great opportunity, not only to cover history, but to dive deeper into the driving forces behind the historic events to be covered. It also came to my mind that I could now write about something that has always bothered me...

In my own lifetime I've been taught many different things about 'where democracy came from': first I was told the Magna Carta, then the Greeks, and in some form or fashion the American Revolution and the Declaration of Independence entered the field, along with the great minds and writings of those like George Buchanan, John Locke and Thomas Paine.

This always bothered me, the fact that we had no definitive understanding of the 'birth' of something that is so part and parcel of our lives, and is mentioned on a more than regular basis in the media, the political arena, and our schools.

Over the years I considered the following...

The Greeks developed a well-known system of self-government, but excluded women (as an inferior breed) from positions of decision-making in the ruling class, and of course the slave population was included in this sub-level category as well. So where is the equality?

The Magna Carta was an attempt to 'level the playing field' for the people that were living under the rule of the all-powerful kings and queens, in a feudal system. The realisation of the apparent faults existing within this system gave way to the writing of the Magna Carta, but this document is still embedded in the system of serfs and lords, masters and servants. And though it tries to equalise the rights of the common man with those of their rulers, the class system was too strong, and the language in the document too weak, to really bring forth this 'equality for all'.

Through my study of the Celtic culture, some things became obvious to me after a while. There seemed to be a particular theme running through not only the history, but the folklore and cultural belief system that was different. A quality so subtle it could easily be overlooked... an underlying equality of all.

It's there in the very way people speak to each other, in the social order, ethics and self-image, in the history, folk stories, songs and mythology. And it's been there for a very, very long time.

It's a woman who wears the mantle of being the progenitor of the Scots people. Scota was her name, and her husband's name is not often mentioned. But she is there, even in the Declaration of Arbroath; nothing sub-level about women from the get-go with this race of people.

And as for the Picts, the other cultural people who inhabited

Scotland's shores, their system of inheritance and of rule is believed to have been passed through the line of women. Within this Scots/Pictish culture, many stories have been passed down of female warriors, leaders and advisers.

Many, to this very day, will say, 'the feudal system of rule reigned over the Middle Ages throughout the Western world.' But in Scotland, the clan systems that descended from the Celtic and Pictish tribes still held the power. Within this realm, the chiefs were not 'rulers' in the feudal sense, but were considered to be the 'first among equals'. There was a bloodline connection between the chieftain/ chieftainess and the people they viewed as their clan. Not so in the feudal world, where through treachery or war the throne could and often did fall into the hands of a foreign power.

Those same clans were once again to rise up as late as the 1600s and 1700s, to bring their 'chosen king' back to the throne. They all carried within them, in their hearts and their spirits, that long-held belief in equality and the rights that each person is given at birth.

These ideals of basic rights for all go back through millennia; the right to be involved in the choice of leadership, the code of ethics contained within the code of Highland hospitality, and the general way of life. And these same ideals, held fast by the Scots, have helped to deliver up to us our freedom.

The freedom that we take for granted today was given to us by the sacrifice and endurance of those that came before. This freedom, and the democracy that grew from it, was over 500 years in the making.

This book will take you from the days of William Wallace and Robert the Bruce during the Wars of Independence in Scotland, to the days of George Washington and Thomas Jefferson and their fight for freedom in America during the Revolutionary War. Follow the thread from Scotland to America, and come to understand how important one ended up being to the other.

We will see how and why a 'wordsmith' (writer) in Arbroath, Scotland, created a document in 1320... and the influence it had 450 years later, and thousands of miles away, on a new people, in a new land.

On 20 January 2009, having just been sworn in, President Barack Obama spoke the following passages in his Inauguration Address:

> Our Founding Fathers, faced with perils that we can scarcely imagine, drafted a charter to assure the rule of law and the rights of man – a charter expanded by the blood of generations. Those ideals still light the world, and we will not give them up... We are the keepers of this legacy... America: Let it be said by our children's children that when we were tested we refused to let this journey end, that we did not turn back nor did we falter... we carried forth that great gift of freedom and delivered it safely to future generations.

Though centuries have passed, we can clearly see the ideals surrounding the basic 'Rights of Man' contained in the history covered in this book have not been set aside nor lost along the way, but are still in the forefront of mankind's needs, and weigh heavily on the minds of many leaders today.

LINDA MACDONALD-LEWIS,
MAY 2009

SCOTLAND

THE WARS OF INDEPENDENCE

To understand how the Declaration of Arbroath came about, and why it went on to have such an influence on America's Declaration of Independence, we need to go back to the 13th century.

1 TRAGEDY COMES ON THE WIND

SCOTLAND FARED AS well as any country in the 13th century.

Most of the old troubles of Viking raids and invasions with the Norsemen had come to a close under the rule of Alexander III, and a treaty was signed at Perth in 1266.

Alexander had been married to Princess Margaret (daughter of Henry III of England) since he was 10 years old. They had been betrothed in early childhood, and married two years after his inauguration as king (at the age of eight), upon the death of his father at Scone in 1249.

Sadly, Margaret passed away in 1275, leaving Alexander with one daughter, also named Margaret, who in 1281 was married to Eric II of Norway. In 1283 she too died, while giving birth to a daughter, again named Margaret, who became known as the 'Maid of Norway'.

It is said in the Lanercost Chronicle that Alexander did not spend many of his widowed days alone:

> he used never to forebear on account of season nor storm, nor for perils of flood or rocky cliffs, but would visit none too creditably nuns or matrons, virgins or widows as the fancy seized him, sometimes in disguise.

This trait of paying little mind to danger in the pursuit of a woman, as we will see, was to take a heavy toll on his future.

In 1285 Alexander married again, this time to a young and vital woman, Yolande of Dureux, daughter of the Comte de Dureux, of France.

At the same time, there was a very well-known figure

named 'Thomas the Rhymer' in Scotland, also known as 'True Thomas' because he was bound to always speak the truth. Thomas, according to legend, had once been out on the hillside playing his harp when he encountered a beautiful woman, whom he thought to be an angel from heaven. And he said: 'All hail, thou mighty Queen of Heaven! For thy peer on earth I never did see.'

This beauty answered, 'Oh no, oh no, Thomas', she said. 'For I am the queen of fair Elphame, that am come hither to visit thee.' ('Elphame' meaning Elfland, Elf's Home or Faeryland.)

She took him on a wild adventure through many lands and into the faery realm, where he was told not to speak a word. He stayed there with her for seven years. When he emerged back into the world of mankind, he had the remarkable gifts of prophecy and poetry. His fame and the story of his disappearance and return with these faery gifts soon spread throughout the land.

On 18 March 1286, it is recorded that Thomas the Rhymer spoke these words:

> Alas for the morrow, day of misery and calamity! Before the hour of noon there will assuredly be felt such a mighty storm in Scotland that its like has not been known for long ages past. The blast of it will cause nations to tremble, will make those who hear it dumb, and will humble the high, and lay the strong level with the ground.

I'm sure everyone that heard this statement must have wondered, 'what does this all mean?'

It wasn't long before it became obvious to all.

On that very same day, 18 March, Alexander was away from his home in Kinghorn, where his young bride awaited him. A storm brewed in the skies. In his rush to return to the royal manor, he laid his better judgment aside and did not heed the warnings of those around him to wait for the storm to pass, but rushed on.

At the ferry crossing at Dalmeny, Alexander persuaded the ferryman to take him across the waters, even though it was dangerous crossing in the violent weather that was at hand. It is said that when Alexander asked this ferryman if he was afraid to die, the man replied, 'I would be honoured, and could do no worse, than to share in the fate of your father's son.' They made the crossing and arrived without mishap at the other side. So they pushed onward, Alexander and his small band of men, toward Kinghorn.

Somehow, Alexander was separated from his men in the stormy weather that night. The next day the ill-fated king was found at the bottom of a cliff, dead, with a broken neck. The belief was that his horse must have thrown him, to tumble down the cliff to his destined demise. And all agreed it was an accident.

And so the king's habit of throwing caution to the wind, and Thomas the Rhymer's prediction that day, came together... in a storm that would continue to blow through Scotland for many years to come, and threaten the very survival of the nation.

2 THE STRUGGLE FOR THE CROWN

WITH THE DEATH of Alexander III, as with the passing of any king that has no living son, a debate began to decide where the 'rightful heir' to the throne and crown could be found. (First there was a wait, to see if the late king's wife, Yolande, was carrying his unborn child: she was not. Yolande disappears from the records here, and is never mentioned in Scotland's history again.) Anyone that had any connection in their bloodline to the crown stepped forward. The families of Bruce, Balliol and Comyn all brought out their documents and tried to prove their case, each striving to show that they had the best claim. The legal debate went on for quite some time, with no conclusion.

Then, in 1290, a solution was offered by the Treaty of Birgham. This treaty proposed that the Maid of Norway (Margaret, Alexander III's granddaughter) should marry the future King of England, Edward II (Edward I's son). The Maid of Norway was heir to the Norwegian throne, and it was established that she was next in line for the Scottish throne as well. (Could this have been Edward I of England's initial attempt at gaining control of Scotland, through the marriage of his son?)

The young girl was sent for, and travelled to Scotland to claim the throne. Unfortunately, the child had been sickly ever since birth, and she died in Orkney while en route, never making it to the mainland.

Edward I, called 'Longshanks' (because of his long legs and height), and later known as the 'Hammer of the Scots', comes into the picture here.

Longshanks had taken possession of the Isle of Man, which had been given to Alexander III in the treaty with the Norse. He had also invaded Wales, and had pretty much taken over there as well... so what came next appears rather strange.

It seems that in an act of desperation, so that some solution to the problem of the empty throne could be found, Edward I was invited into the debate by the Scottish nobility.

Edward must have been delighted by the news, and he believed it only right 'that a king should choose a king'.

After Edward's scholars and advisers looked at all of the documentation and heard all of the arguments, they returned their findings to him. The decision was made that John Balliol had the most direct link, and would take the position of King of Scotland. Many say that this was a strategic move on Longshanks' part, because Balliol was easily influenced and would do whatever Longshanks told him. Later Balliol would be referred to as the 'Toom Tabard', which meant the 'Empty Garment'; more commonly he was known as the 'Puppet King'.

John Balliol was crowned King of Scotland at Scone on 30 November 1292, St Andrew's Day.

It must have been a hard position for Balliol to be in; every time he did what Edward I wanted, it upset his own people, and every time he sided with Scotland, he upset Edward I. When Longshanks demanded that the Scots rally their men to fight for England against France, it was the proverbial last straw, and Balliol knew he could no longer stay in this odd position. The leaders of Scotland also knew this, and formed a council of their own, a panel of 'Guardians of Scotland'.

In 1295 the Guardians turned away from Longshanks and their king's fealty to him, and agreed to an alliance with France. This was the beginning of what is referred to as the 'Auld Alliance'. The agreement was that Scotland would aid France against England, and France would aid Scotland against England – or 'the common enemy'.

3 LONGSHANKS PICKS UP THE HAMMER

EDWARD I WAS none too pleased by these events, and no doubt felt threatened by the new alliance between Scotland and France. His reaction was to invade Scotland. This started what would be known as the 'Scottish Wars of Independence'.

On 30 March 1296, Edward the Longshanks marched his massive army into Berwick-upon-Tweed and massacred the town in the most dreadful way. The carnage went on for three days, the 'Tweed ran red with blood' and acts of pure savagery were carried out by Edward's men. No man, woman or child was spared the sword or spear. And Berwick, a once thriving port town, never recovered its full economic strength again.

Then, four short weeks later, on 27 April, the Scots army met the English at Dunbar, and the Scots were defeated. Many Scots nobles were taken to England as hostages.

Edward didn't stop there; his army moved north through Edinburgh and Stirling, and he gathered up Scotland's treasures along the way: documents, lands, records and religious artefacts. Probably the most noted piece in Edward's plunder was the Stone of Scone, or Stone of Destiny. This stone, which sat at Scone Palace in Perth, was used in the coronation of Scottish kings. The legend was that the 'rightful king' to Scotland would be welcomed by it, but if 'one not right' sat on it... it would cry out. It was also said that wherever the Stone lay, so did the ruling power of Scotland... maybe that's why Edward wanted it. He had it placed at Westminster Abbey, under the coronation throne there. (The stone was returned to Scotland in 1996 and is now on display at Edinburgh Castle, with the other treasures of Scotland. Elizabeth II was the latest monarch crowned sitting above the stone, in 1952.)

Balliol was captured by Edward I on 8 July 1296, and stripped of his mantle as King of Scotland. Scotland was once again without a king.

Edward the Longshanks continued to tighten his grip on the Scots and on Scotland. He appointed the Earl of Warenne (the victor of Dunbar) as the 'keeper' or viceroy of Scotland,

and a man named Hugh Cressingham as the treasurer. Then he demanded that all the Scottish lords come to Berwick and sign a document that stated Edward was now the 'Overlord of Scotland'.

This document became known as the 'Ragman Rolls', referring to the ribbons on which the lords' seals were attached. It's been said that the word 'rigmarole' which can mean 'a time wasting procedure' might have come from the Ragman Rolls. When men are forced to sign and seal a document against their own will, it becomes a meaningless waste of time. This 'roll' has played an important part in charting Scotland's history, because it plainly lists the great family names in residence in Scotland in the 13th century.

It must be noted here as well that you'll not find the names of William Wallace, nor his brother Malcolm, included on the Ragman Rolls. (Was this the first public sign of their resistance to Longshanks, and their heartfelt patriotism toward their homeland?)

Statue of 'The Wee Wallace' by Handyside Ritchie, 1859, Stirling
Image courtesy of the Stirling Smith Art Gallery and Museum

4 THE WALLACE AND HIS MIGHTY SWORD

Freedom is best, I tell thee true
of all things to be won
Then never live within
the bond of slavery, my son.

THIS OLD RHYME is a Latin proverb that is said to have been taught to a young William Wallace by his uncle to show him the true value of freedom. History proves that this lesson was heard well and taken to heart by the young lad, and these words reflect the ideals held by Wallace for the rest of his life.

We don't know a lot about William Wallace's early life... Was he born in 1270, 1274 or 1276? Was he born in Ellerslie or Elderslie? Was he an outlaw or a common man just trying to live out his life in peace and freedom? Some of these questions may never be answered... and we won't debate any of that, here.

What we do know about Wallace has come down through some historic documentation, but mostly through legends and stories that have been passed from generation to generation.

There is also an epic poem, written by a bard named Blind Harry during the 1470s, commonly called *Blind Harry's Wallace*. It was printed in 1508, and went through over 20 editions between then and 1707. In 1722, it was translated by William Hamilton of Gilbertfield into modern Scots from old Scots. He titled the updated Scots version, 'The Life and Heroick Actions of the renoun'd Sir William Wallace, General and Governour of Scotland'. This version was republished in 1998[1], so it is easily obtainable, and can still be read today.

And of course, the character of William Wallace was depicted in the movie *Braveheart*, written by Randall Wallace and released in 1995, which had great impact on the world[2].

---

[1] *Blind Harry's Wallace*, William Hamilton of Gilbertfield, edited by Elspeth King (Luath Press, Edinburgh, 1998)

[2] More can be read about this movie's global effect in Lin Anderson's book, *Braveheart: From Hollywood to Holyrood* (Luath Press, Edinburgh, 2005)

A note of caution here... the story of Wallace in the movie has been embellished a bit, in a typically Hollywood way... but it is still well worth the viewing. The movie does capture the atmosphere of the day, and Wallace's uncompromising nature in his fight to free his country from the grasp of the English. It is well acted, and a moving story of a great hero that anyone can enjoy... whether they have connections to Scotland or not.

It is possible that Wallace was on the field of battle at Dunbar. He was old enough then, but no one knows for sure. He really enters our history with the killing of the Sheriff of Lanark, named Hesilrig, in May 1297, in retaliation for the senseless murder of his wife, Marion Braidfoot (called 'Murron' in *Braveheart*). We may never know if Wallace really did have a wife, or if this was really her name. But this is what has come down through the stories about him. According to Blind Harry, after the killing of Hesilrig, Wallace swore he would kill any and all English that were old enough to raise arms against Scotland from then on.

There are some interesting stories about Wallace prior to the killing included in *Blind Harry's Wallace*. Here's two of those:

He once killed a lad in Dundee who thought Wallace was wearing clothes of too fine a quality for a Scot. When the lad tried to relieve Wallace of his knife, Wallace dispatched him promptly, and had to flee Dundee. The lad he'd killed was the son of a local English constable.

When Wallace was out fishing on the Irvine Water, a group of English soldiers tried to take his catch. Wallace offered them a share of the fish, but when one soldier demanded the whole catch and drew his sword, Wallace knocked him down with his fishing-net and grabbed the sword for himself. He killed three of the five soldiers, and two escaped. When the two escapees told their lord, named Percy, of the incident, he replied, 'if one Scot can take down three of my soldiers and put the remaining two to flight, then I will not pursue such a man as this any further.'

These stories have only come down to us because of the

further actions of Wallace, sparked by the love of his home-land and freedom. But these sorts of things must have been happening to many Scots throughout the land, so it isn't hard to see why so many rallied to Wallace's side when the call came to take a stance against such oppression.

And so the legend of Wallace starts. He was seen as an out-law and a thief by the invading English, and as an uncompromising hero by the local Scots. Regardless of what is written today to praise or discredit Wallace, it is obvious that he was able to inspire those of all ranks. Throughout Scotland, from the common man to the titled, Wallace's inspiration led them to fight for the freedom of their nation.

Rebellion started to break out in Scotland. Wallace fought at Loudoun Hill victoriously, and again in Ayr. He fought alongside Sir William Douglas at Scone. Then the nobles of Scotland agreed to terms with the English, at Irvine in July 1297. This was a hard thing to accept for those who had been fighting against the English invasion. So Wallace and his fol-lowers joined Andrew de Moray's army at Stirling in August. De Moray had successfully started his own rebellion, and the two armies met up and prepared to take the English in battle.

Linocut by Owain Kirby, The Battle of Stirling Bridge – courtesy of the Stirling Smith Art Gallery and Museum

The Battle of Stirling Bridge

On 11 September 1297, even though outnumbered, the Scots had their day of victory against the forces of Edward, the Hammer of the Scots, and his army.

There were 10,000 men of infantry and 300 cavalry on the English side that day who gathered and came to cross the Stirling Bridge, to enter the field for battle. But Wallace and de Moray weren't going to play out the day by known battle-field rules...

In a brilliant move on the part of the Scots, they allowed a portion of the English army to cross the bridge, then started the attack. The narrow width of the bridge would not allow more than maybe three men abreast to cross at a time. So after the Scots had dealt with those on their side of the river, they easily dispatched the others as they crossed. The confusion and panic must have been overwhelming, as some parts of the English army tried to retreat back onto the bridge, while others still marched forward. The bridge is said to have collapsed under the weight of it, and many drowned.

There is a legend that Wallace had one of his men go under the bridge and cut through the underpinning of the structure. The man inserted a pin to hold the bridge in place until the signal came from Wallace to remove it... and that's what caused

Old postcard – courtesy of the Stirling Smith Art Gallery and Museum

the collapse of the bridge that day. This may be true, as Wallace was known for his strategy and genius in battle.

Wallace is also said to have killed Hugh Cressingham that day, and to have come back to his corpse at the end of the battle, flayed the skin from it, and used it to make a belt for his mighty sword.

The victory was sweet, and a grand boost to the confidence of the Scots in their fight for freedom. Wallace was knighted, and he and de Moray were named as 'Guardians of Scotland and Leaders of its Armies'. Some say that Robert the Bruce himself could have conducted these ceremonies, but once again there is no documentation of this.

Andrew de Moray received terrible wounds on the battle-field at Stirling Bridge, and subsequently died from them a couple of months later in November 1297. This left Wallace the sole Guardian of Scotland.

The Battle of Falkirk and the Fall of Wallace

On 22 July 1298, Edward's army met up with Wallace again, at Falkirk, but this time with terrible results for the Scots. Their blood flowed freely onto the battlefield in this defeat. Wallace, however, escaped.

Scottish leaders' confidence in Wallace started to fade after this. By September of that year, he had resigned from being Guardian of Scotland.

Wallace is said to have gone to France, supposedly to seek aid from the people there for the struggle in Scotland. (In the past this was debated, and there seemed to be no documentation of his journeying there. But recently an online petition has been asking for the safe return of an artefact that was among the personal effects of William Wallace when he was captured at Robroyston. The petition asks the National Archives, Kew, for the return of the 'Safe Conduct Letter from King of France Philip IV (reference number SC 1/30 m.81) carried by Sir William Wallace on his capture at Robroyston, 3 August 1305' and states that it is now lying in a drawer in London. The once-doubted story that Wallace went to France seems to be confirmed by this item's recent rediscovery. It is something that really should be returned to Scotland for public viewing and educational purposes.)

Meanwhile, Edward offered ransom and bribes to any that could bring the outlaw Wallace to him. Wallace avoided capture until 3 August 1305, when he was betrayed by Sir John de Menteith at Robroyston and turned over to the English. He was taken to London, arriving on 22 August. His trial was held the next morning. He was found guilty of being a traitor to Edward I and of the murder of Heselrig, to name just a couple of the charges. Wallace stated that he could not be a traitor to Edward, because Edward was not his king, but this statement fell on deaf ears.

On 23 August 1305, William Wallace was literally dragged through the streets of London to Smithfield and slaughtered. After torturous acts were committed on his body, he was killed and then beheaded. They cut off his arms and legs, then sent them to four strategic sites, Newcastle, Berwick, Stirling and Perth, as a warning to the people that they would meet the same end if they acted against Edward.

When Wallace was captured in 1305, he did not have his sword with him. It is said it was taken to Dumbarton Castle (known as 'The Rock') and stored there. This sword is almost five and a half feet long from pommel to tip. It is now on display at the Wallace Monument located on the Abbey Craig, where Wallace mustered his troops for the Battle of Stirling Bridge. If you are ever in this part of Scotland, the Stirling area is a must see. So many historic events happened there. Stirling Castle, Stirling Bridge, the Wallace Monument, Bannockburn Field and the Smith Art Gallery and Museum (where many Wallace artefacts are kept) are all within easy reach of the town.

I had a hand-folded, hand-crafted replica of Wallace's sword made for me in Scotland. I keep it on display in the shop, so people can see for themselves its grand and forceful potential as a battle weapon. One can only imagine the enormous size and strength of the man that wielded it in so many battles. It is indeed a mighty sword.

Here's an item of interest... All the bodies of water in Scotland are called 'lochs', yet one is named 'lake'... 'Lake of Menteith'. I was told they would never give it a Gaelic name, 'for sins, yet unpaid [by Sir John de Menteith], for betraying Wallace'. Others say it's called 'lake' because of a mistake a mapmaker made centuries ago in the listing of it. If so, it seems a bit strange that it's never been corrected.

I've also heard it said that Menteith's act of betrayal was one of the deepest known because Wallace was the godfather to some of Menteith's younger family members.

A very detailed account of the life and legend of William Wallace is available for a further study of this heroic man. *On the Trail of William Wallace* by David R. Ross[3] is very well

---

3 Luath Press, Edinburgh, 1999

written and easy to follow, and includes maps pinpointing where the key events of Wallace's life took place. It can easily be used as a guide through Scotland's countryside while touring.

David R. Ross is the convener of the Society of William Wallace in Scotland, and a man I feel honoured to know and call a friend. He has dedicated his life to his beloved home-land of Scotland, and to keeping the actions and history of its great heroes alive. I have watched him for over a decade now, literally 'going the extra mile' to organise events, preserve historic sites and keep the lessons learned from Scotland's past in the forefront of the public's mind. This is an important thing in these present days. Scots are once again embracing the ideals of their ancestors, questioning their present form of government and debating openly the path of their future, in a way not seen in many other countries today. (Northern Ireland, having just recently brought an end to the Troubles, is another realm that comes to mind.)

2005 marked the 700th anniversary of the capture and execution of William Wallace by the English, and David organised many events in Scotland and England to mark the occasion. Preparing for one of these events took him at least four years, spent gaining the physical endurance to complete the 'Walk for Wallace': leaving Robroyston (where Wallace was captured by the English in 1305) on 3 August 2005, David walked the approximately 450 miles to London in the same 19 days it took Wallace to get there. This was a remarkable achievement, for anyone. He arrived on 22 August... but it didn't stop there.

The next day (23 August) David led the huge mass of people that had arrived from all over the world to honour Wallace. This parade of men and women, clad in tartan, beating drums and playing bagpipes, marched six miles through London, along the very route that Wallace had taken to his place of execution.

Shortly thereafter, the first funeral ever held for Sir William Wallace took place at Saint Bartholomew the Great Church, close by Smithfield, where Wallace breathed his last.

A special coffin was made for the occasion. People worldwide sent selected items and personal inscriptions about Wallace, which were placed inside the coffin in lieu of his remains. I suppose that is actually what does remain of 'The Wallace': his undying inspiration to all that have come in contact with his life and legend.

Thanks David, for all you've done and continue to do for Scotland.

A full account of these events can be read in David's book, *For Freedom: the Last Days of William Wallace* (Luath Press, Edinburgh, 2005).

5 ROBERT THE BRUCE TAKES UP THE FIGHT

No man holds his flesh and blood in hatred
and I am no exception.
I must join my own people
and the nation in which I was born.

ROBERT THE BRUCE is said to have spoken these words to the Knights of Annandale (aligned with his father), who considered themselves to be Edward's men. This statement may have had little effect on them, but it was the sign that the younger Bruce was taking a stance in the struggle with the English.

The future King of Scots, Robert I, was born at Turnberry Castle in 1274. He was of both Celtic and Norman descent; his title, the Earl of Carrick, came to him from his mother's line, and his claim to the throne of Scotland came from his father's.

Bruce no doubt felt frustration at the decision that Balliol would take the crown. The three main contenders, the families of Comyn, Bruce and Balliol, had made violent moves against each other during the struggle for the claim of the throne. Those actions left a mark on Bruce that would have a strong influence on his life and on the future of Scotland.

After the defeat at Falkirk, when Wallace stepped down from the position of Guardian of Scotland, the Bruce and John 'the Red' Comyn were made joint Guardians. Comyn was a nephew to Balliol, and his hard and fast supporter. Putting him and Bruce together like this seems strange, as they were none too fond of each other. Politically it made sense to honour the two other families closest to the crown, but politics is rarely based on common sense.

The friction between Bruce and Comyn was so intense that within a year (in 1299) William Lamberton, the Bishop of St Andrews, was appointed as a third Guardian (or referee). Then, in 1300, Bruce resigned from his post, and was replaced by Sir Gilbert, First Lord of Umfraville and Earl of Angus.

By 1302, Edward I's actions in Scotland showed little results, and a nine-month truce was enacted between England and Scotland. He began his invasions once more in 1303, this time with much better results, and once again the tide turned against the Scots. By 1304 all of the powerful men in Scotland had submitted to Edward, except one... William Wallace. John 'the Red' Comyn negotiated the surrender. This act on Comyn's part furthered the disdain for him felt by many of the patriots of Scotland.

Seeing how things had gone and were going for their country, the Bruce and Lamberton made between them a secret pact, an 'alliance against all men'. Edward was old and very ill, so they waited, knowing the political arena would change drastically with his passing. Meanwhile, Longshanks acted rapidly to move the political power of Scotland below the border, to England.

The Seed of Discontent

Robert the Bruce and his family held the belief that their claim to the crown was the best, but of course the Comyn and Balliol families would have been of the same mindset. The Bruce, unlike the Red Comyn, had teetered between support of his homeland and the English king's court. This cast doubt on him and his motives among both the common men and the nobles of his country.

John Comyn was more steadfast in his loyalties. He was related, in one way or another, to most of the powerful families on both sides of the border. But Comyn had committed his own questionable acts, which must be pointed out. At Falkirk, Comyn had led his men off the field of battle at a crucial point, in what some claim was an act of betrayal, not only to Wallace, but to Scotland. This act was seen as the turning point of the battle, which caused the defeat of the Scots that day. As if that was not bad enough, in 1299, after the crushing defeat at Falkirk, when Wallace left the country, Comyn stated that he had done so without the permission of the Guardians, and that because of this the Wallaces must forfeit their lands into the Comyns' hands. William's brother Malcolm Wallace was having none of that, and drew his sword, as did the Comyn. The Bruce came to Malcolm's aid and the Red

Comyn grabbed Robert by the throat. These kinds of situation do not fade from the memory very fast.

Some may say that stories like these are not true or cannot be proven. I think the stories are there to depict the state of affairs during that particular time in history. They may now be considered to be 'nothing more than a myth', but all myths are sewn with the thread of truth, though embellished, and that's the point. Stories such as these show the ill feelings that led to the next event.

Murder at the Altar

In 1305 William Wallace was captured and executed.

The Bruce believed the only way to stop the force of Edward in Scotland was for the Red Comyn and himself to band together. They fell into an agreement that the Bruce would take the crown of Scotland, and John 'the Red' Comyn would take the Bruce's lands and holdings as his own. The Bruce thought this agreement was binding, until he was in London and heard of the Red Comyn's plot to betray him, by telling Edward of the arrangement.

Upon hearing this news, Edward immediately called a parliament to session, and Bruce was summoned. He came, unaware of the Red Comyn's treachery. Edward produced the document of agreement between Bruce and Comyn, with the seals attached, and asked Bruce if he knew of it and had attached his own seal to it. The Bruce said he would, by the king's agreement, take one day to consider the document, and would return the next day with it intact, and he made a pledge of his lands to the king as a kind of collateral. Edward agreed, believing he had the upper hand in the situation.

When he left, the Bruce rushed back to Scotland. And the story goes... at the Borders he met a man he believed to be a messenger, and when he searched him he found yet another document being sent to Edward from the Comyn, calling for the immediate, secure confinement and detention, or the speedy execution of the Bruce, in light of the treacherous acts being carried out by him. The Bruce and his men retrieved the document and beheaded the man, then thanked God for His guidance in the fortunate event of meeting that messenger. Then Bruce heard that John Comyn was staying in Dumfries, and made haste there.

10 February 1306, Bruce found John Comyn at Greyfriar's monastery in front of the high altars. No one is sure what passed between the two inside the church that day. The bad blood that had flowed between them for years was soon to be spilled.

One can only imagine the Bruce asking Comyn if their agreement still held firm: when the Comyn wavered in his stance, the Bruce, knowing of his treachery, became enraged. He pulled out the newfound documents with the Comyn's seal on them, which Comyn believed to be on their way to Edward. Bruce then proceeded to draw his weapon and strike a heavy blow.

It's said that the Bruce then rushed from the building and made his way to his horse in the cemetery entrance. He was met by his kinsmen, who, seeing the state of the Bruce, asked how it had gone. Bruce said to Sir Roger de Kirkpatrick, 'I doubt I have slain the Comyn'.

Kirkpatrick responded, 'I'll mak sikker!' (I'll make sure!), and went with John Lindsay into the church, where the monks were aiding the badly wounded but still living Comyn. Seeing him alive, and thinking he might recover, the men struck the fatal blow, finishing the traitor off. Robert Comyn, John's brother, rushed to his defence and was dispatched by Bruce's men as well.

The circumstances surrounding this act have been debated for centuries. Who was the traitor, the Bruce or John Comyn? Was Bruce doing no more than clearing the deck for his own claim to the throne? Was John Comyn the more suitable man for leadership in Scotland? Did Comyn deserve death as justice for his treacherous ways?

These things can only be debated, and really no satisfactory conclusion can be found to the debate. The history is what it is... a mixture of written documents (which are no doubt influenced by political mindsets) and folklore (the stories that the common folk chose to believe, to justify their own feelings about events of then-recent history, which were further used to inspire the young and bring comfort to the old). We also know today that 10 people watching the same event unfold will give you 10 different versions of what happened. Eye witness accounts cannot always be relied on.

The life of Robert the Bruce became very complicated at this point. He had not only committed an act of murder within a church building, but had made mortal enemies of the Comyns, their supporters, and King Edward 1, all in one swift blow. Many of those that had once supported his efforts now turned away from him.

The Bruce rode on to Glasgow and made confession of his brutal act to Bishop Wishart, who gave him absolution for his crime.

The plans were laid for Robert the Bruce to be crowned as King of Scots.

Statue of King Robert the Bruce at Bannockburn Battlefield by Pilkington Jackson, unveiled June 1964
Image courtesy of the Stirling Smith Art Gallery and Museum

6 THE CORONATION OF THE KING AND THE BATTLE OF BANNOCKBURN

A FEW SHORT weeks later, Robert the Bruce was crowned King of Scots, on 25 March 1306. The ceremony was conducted in private, with only a few in attendance. The Bruce did not keep it a secret though, but quickly wrote to Edward I, demanding recognition as Scotland's king.

Longshanks was none too pleased. He wrote to the Pope, Clement V, to inform him of the murder of John Comyn, the 'treasonous' documents and the fact that Bruce had made himself King of Scotland. The Pope excommunicated the Bruce from the Church, and Edward the Longshanks made plans to renew his invasion of Scotland.

These two things – Bruce's excommunication and Edward's renewed invasion of Scotland – led to the events that were eventually to have a deep effect on the forming of the Scottish nation; and of another nation, many miles away and hundreds of years later.

With Longshanks on the move to Scotland, by way of Nottingham (he was there by July), Bruce knew he had to gather support. This was no easy task. Many that once had lent their support to his efforts had been put off by the murder of John 'the Red' Comyn. Much of his support came now from those that lived on his own lands, like the Earls of Lennox, Mar and Atholl.

The Earl of Pembroke, Edward's man, advanced to Perth, captured Bishop Wishart and took Lamberton by surrender. Things did not look good for Scotland's new King Robert. The Battle of Methven was a disaster for him; many of his men were taken, some were executed and some turned to the English for mercy, and took a stand against the Bruce. King Robert moved westward to gather support from the MacDonalds and was attacked in Lorne by Highland men, the MacDougalls. Soon Robert's family became the targets; his brother Neil was captured and executed, by being hanged, drawn and beheaded. Of the Bruce's female family members that were taken by the English, two were hung in cages on the towers of Berwick and Roxburgh, while others were imprisoned or sent off to convents, and Robert's Queen Elizabeth was imprisoned in a royal manor at Burstwick-in-Holderness. The Earl of Atholl was captured while trying to keep safe these same womenfolk, and was hanged.

This news must have worn heavily on the king's mind and heart. His support had been split by his own actions at Greyfriar's monastery, the English were gaining strength in Scotland, he'd not been victorious in a battle and his family and friends had suffered because of him and his campaign. Depression was a likely scenario, to say the least, and it's said that at this time he took refuge in the Western Highlands and Islands.

It's during this time that the legend of 'The Bruce and the Spider' is said to have happened.

I read this legend for the first time as a young child, in a book called *Stories and Songs from Many Lands* (University Society Incorporated, New York, 1955). The version in that book was written by Graeme MacDonald, but the story has been penned by countless authors down through the years, and I've read many of them.

Here's my version:

Poor King Robert had gone to a remote area to hide from the opposing forces and save his own life. Wandering through the forests, in the mountains, for days on end, he was hungry, cold and tired. One day he came across a lonely wooden hut tucked away in the woods. It was empty, so he went inside to shelter himself and lay down in despair.

'There's no reason to continue on,' he thought, 'so many have suffered already because of me and my dream, and I'm not making any progress against the forces of the English. My country and my people are at risk of losing all. I should just give up. Six times I have tried to push back the English and six times I have failed. Six battles behind me and six failures, why should I try again?'

Now just as he was thinking this, he saw a small spider spinning a long thread to create a web. This spider swung on the thread, trying to attach it to a beam of wood to secure the start of its new home. The wind blew in and the thread broke free, dropping the poor little creature to the floor of the hut. Robert watched as the spider climbed back up the wall to the ceiling and started the process again. Once more the spider dangled from the thread and swung toward the beam, and once more it was knocked to the floor. Again the spider crept up to the ceiling and started the pattern over.

Robert was glad for the distraction from his own worries and watched this unfold with great wonder. Again the spider tried and failed and again it scampered across the floor and up the wall to the ceiling to make another attempt.

'What strength and determination this little beastie has,' Robert thought to himself. He was so involved in watching the drama with the spider that he forgot his own troubles.

Again the spider tried and failed. Six times King Robert

watched the spider try its methods, six times he saw the poor spider fail, and six times the little beastie fell to the floor. But the spider did not give up, it just climbed back to the ceiling, positioned itself and began to spin its thread. It spun and spun the thread to the right length, then swung toward the beam... and this time, it worked. The spider secured the base of its home and started its work to build it.

King Robert stood up and said 'Hoorah! Good sir... you have done it!' and bowed grandly to the little spider. 'You sir, have taught me a great lesson today, to never give up! You did not give up on your home, no matter how many times you failed. And I sir will do the same... I will not give up!'

The great King Robert was inspired and found a strength in his body he'd not felt in a very long time. He stood, straightened his sword, picked up his shield and left the little hut. He gathered up his scattered army of warriors, met the English army for battle, and on the seventh try he won. He went on to free his country and reign over it, bringing in ideals of democracy that were to influence the world from then on.

The moral to the story of course is... 'if at first you don't succeed, try, try again.'

Great story... well worth repeating for the next 700 years.

Here's an example of the influence it has even today:

I was at a book launch in Edinburgh a few years ago. A group of us were standing in a circle facing each other and talking about Robert the Bruce, when to our amazement a spider dropped down from the vaulted ceiling, right into the middle of our circle. The talk immediately turned to the story of Bruce and the Spider. We were shocked and amazed as the little thing dangled there in the air between us. Then as the little beastie dropped down to the floor, everyone started to warn those around them to make way for the spider, telling all what had just happened and urging everyone around not to step on it. Soon everyone within the area of the little thing was looking to the floor and talking about the Bruce and the Spider.

I was tickled at the sight of this, and the experience of it as well. Even today, this story has a huge impact on Scotland and its people.

In the spring of 1307, Edward the Longshanks marched North towards Scotland, dispersing Bruce's lands to his followers as he went. He also proclaimed the Bruce's excommunication to all along the way. He captured many of the Bruce's family members at this time, and meted out justice in his own way, caging women and executing men even though they had surrendered.

But by 7 July 1307, Longshanks was dead. This was good news for King Robert, for now he would face the late king's son Edward II, who had the reputation of being a weakling. In March of 1309, Bruce held his first parliament at St Andrews. In 1310 the Bruce was recognised by the clergy as the king, in the Declaration of the Clergy, which nullified the Balliol claim to the throne. That year Edward II gave permission for the commanders in his outposts to negotiate truce with the Bruce. Carlisle, Berwick, Banff, Perth, Ayr and Dundee did so. A general truce held until June.

Edward II had his own political worries south of the border. When it came time for the call to be put out to raise an army, only three of his earls responded. Bruce saw an opportunity in this unrest in England and reacted with a series of raids into English territory.

The struggle continued, Bruce reclaiming lands and fortifications, and Edward II pushing forward where he could, when he could. During the time King Bruce was staking his claim at the Isle of Man, Edward II and his men took Stirling Castle. In 1313 Edward Bruce (Robert's brother) began a siege of the castle, and by midsummer a condition of surrender of Stirling was sent to Edward II. If the castle could not be relieved by King Edward's troops by midsummer the next year (24 June 1314), the commander, Sir Philip de Mowbray, would hand over the castle in Stirling to the Scots. Edward II accepted this, though he doubted he would be able to fulfill the terms because of troubles in his own country. England was on the verge of a civil war. The heavy presence of an English army had not been seen in Scotland for nearly two years. Stirling, known as the 'Gateway to the Highlands', was of the utmost importance to the holding of Scotland, and it would be a political embarrassment to Edward II to lose it.

However, the agreement between Edward Bruce and the commander de Mowbray was set so far ahead that it gave the English ample time to gather forces to try to relieve Stirling. Edward marched his huge army into Scotland, believing that he would destroy the Scottish forces and put an end to their struggle forever. The army that Edward II had gathered was massive, up to 3,000 horse and 17,000 footmen, two to three times the size of the Scots army. Among the English ranks was Sir John Comyn, son of John 'the Red' Comyn, educated in England and present to avenge the murder of his father.

Bruce awaited their arrival at the field of Bannockburn. The Scots were outnumbered by the English, but Bruce still had advantages over them. He knew the layout of the land, and had ample time for the preparation of it. He ordered his men to dig pits with stakes alongside the main entry roads, to force the approaching army to stay on the path chosen by him, and to inflict injury and confusion amongst the ranks of his foes. He had a core band of men that had been fighting alongside him since 1306; they worked together like a well oiled machine, and held each other's trust and confidence in battle. One of these men was his trusted friend James 'the Black' Douglas, a warrior feared by all that met him in battle. Bruce also had the support of the well respected warriors from the Clan Donald (the MacDonalds) of the Western Highlands and Islands. All of the branches of the Clan Donald were in support of Good King Robert, save one... the MacDowalls (or MacDougalls) refused to show, and lost much of their land and many of their titles because of this in the years that followed.

The victories of many battles had hinged on whether the MacDonalds came to the field or not. The Clan Donald was the largest of all the clans in Scotland. It's said they could muster more men for battle, in a shorter period of time, than any clan in Scotland. Their physical size (they were noted for their height and muscular stature), brute force and number of men alone could turn a battle's tide and assure the defeat of the enemy. But they were located in the most remote reaches of Scotland's realm, so had to travel further than most to reach the fields of battle, which normally lay closer to the middle of Scotland's land mass. This was the case at Bannockburn.

As time came for the battle to begin, the MacDonalds were nowhere to be seen, and the Bruce was worried. If the Clan Donald didn't show, he was surely going to be defeated. In the eleventh hour, the first Clan Donald chief crested the hill to descend upon the field. As this chief of the Clan Ranald of MacDonald dismounted from his Highland steed, the Bruce rushed forward, clasped his arm in greeting and said, 'My hope is constant in thee'. This statement became the Clan Ranald's motto from then on. Previously it was 'Gainsay Who Dare', which meant oppose me if you dare. The whole of the Clan Donald was to do so well in the forthcoming battle that they won the right to always be at the right flank of the king; a treasured position, and an honour for which any clan or band of warriors would gladly fight.

Bruce could now begin the battle with a new confidence. He had formed four brigades, each forming a schiltron, a hedgehog shape of long spears. These troops of hedgehogs were taught to move rapidly as one unit, which gave them the ability to turn, shift and reform as they encountered the enemy. The first of the brigades was commanded by Randolph, Earl of Moray, stationed near the church of St Ninians. The king commanded the second, and was located near the entrance to the New Park. His brother Edward commanded the third and the Black Douglas the fourth (for the young Walter Stewart, his cousin, who was nominally in charge). Five hundred horsemen were on the side of the Scots as cavalry, and their infantry was 6,000–9,000 strong.

The first day of battle, Sunday, 23 June, started on an odd note, which became a story told over and over in pubs and later schoolyards for centuries to come. Two of the English commanders had been arguing over who would lead the vanguard for Edward II. Edward made them both joint commanders to quell the competition between them, which seems to have done little good. Sir Henry de Bohun, the nephew of the Earl of Hereford, one of the joint commanders, was riding out in front of the body of the vanguard when he spotted King Robert. Robert was separated from his men and was on a small horse, armed only with his trusted battleaxe. De Bohun saw the opportunity to gain fame for himself and started to charge on his warhorse. Bruce calmly watched this.

Robert the Bruce slays De Bohun at Bannockburn by John Duncan
Image courtesy of the Stirling Smith Art Gallery and Museum

Thundering down on the Bruce, de Bohun readied himself to strike. The Bruce side-stepped his horse from the line of the charge, stood up firmly in the stirrups and brought his mighty battleaxe down on de Bohun with such a force that he cleaved through not only de Bohun's helmet but his whole head, cutting both in two. The force of the blow was such that it is said that de Bohun's horse took several steps before collapsing with its rider.

This story ran like wildfire through the ranks of the Scots army.

When Bruce was scolded by his men for taking such a chance, he said the only regret he had was that he'd splintered the shaft of his battleaxe. The army was so inspired by this that they charged the English to start the battle.

The battle continued and the Scots did well. News came to the Bruce that the English camp was disheartened by the events of the first day, and was not resting well for fear of a night attack by the Scots. Bruce had been thinking of retreating to the hills to seek out a rougher terrain on which to meet the English, but when this news reached him he changed his mind.

Right after daybreak the Scots started their move toward the English. On the approach the Scots knelt in a prayer for the day, their lives and their victory. Edward was said to have asked, 'Will yon Scots fight?... Or do they kneel to ask my mercy?' Ingram de Umfraville responded, 'They ask for mercy... but not from you. To God they pray. For them it's death or victory.'

Many of Edward II's men urged him to not engage in battle, but Edward accused them of cowardice. This enraged the Earl of Gloucester, who promptly mounted his horse and charged.

And so started the second day of battle, on Monday, 24 June 1314.

The battle raged on. The schiltrons in motion, coupled with the layout of the land and the streams, concentrated the English forces in such a way that to manoeuver and fight was hard. If a man fell he was trampled by those around him. The Scots continued their drive and soon the English were on the banks of the waterways, and being pushed in, both horses and men. The size of the English army was now working against them, in the ever tightening field, as the Scots pushed and pushed them further to the brink.

Then, in a strange quirk of fate, the English spotted a group on the horizon. Thinking it was reinforcements for the Scots making their way to the battlefield, the English ranks were struck with fear. Ironically, this group was no more than the mass of camp followers, coming out to watch the battle unfold.

Soon Edward ii was seen fleeing the field... and those in his ranks that could find the opportunity fled as well, now that they'd lost their leader.

Edward went to Stirling Castle and was denied entry. So he left the area, circling around the Scots to the west to escape by a southern route, then turning east. All along James 'the Black' Douglas was chasing him. Edward took refuge at Dunbar Castle, then boarded a ship back to England.

And so the victory at Bannockburn was secured against the force of the mass English army, the size of which was unlike anything that would ever be seen again.

Robert the Bruce, King of Scots, would be considered the greatest Scots leader in battle from then on.

7 AFTER THE BATTLE

THE ENGLISH HAD fled the field of Bannockburn in such haste, they'd left all that they brought behind. This was a great economic boon to Scotland and her new king. Great war machines, weapons, provisions, even the Shield and Privy Seal of England. There were plenty of high-ranking men captured, so Robert could use them in ransom to seek the return of friends and family members being held in England.

Victory was sweet for the Scots... in Scotland. But it had little effect on the political arena outside their own borders.

Robert held parliament in Cambuskenneth on 6 November 1314. He put forth a document that stated that those who held lands in both Scotland and England would now have to make a choice as to where their loyalties lay, and which king their allegiance would be given to. To secure their lands in Scotland they must let go their lands in England; if they refused to release their lands in England they would lose those in Scotland. This seemed to be a good way to eliminate the problem of split loyalty, and the shifting of support from one realm to the other. And he had no doubt considered the common man living on these lands, who was called upon to fight on whichever side the landowner supported, often finding himself facing his own countrymen.

Of course, those landowners affected did not view their loss of wealth with much enthusiasm.

Bruce gave them one year to make their choice and register the lands to be claimed. This led to the problem of 'the disinherited': although the landowner of the day may have agreed to Bruce's terms, often their descendants took issue with this, claiming that their lands had been taken under duress and during conditions of war, and demanding their return.

In this decree at Cambuskenneth, Bruce tried to unite Scotland, both clan chiefs and feudal barons and earls, and bring all Scots to common ground, to put their interest in and on their own countrymen and country.

Now you would think all that had happened would have brought an end to the struggle between Scotland and England, but sadly it did not. Edward II wanted Scotland for himself. The defeat at Bannockburn was an embarrassment to him and his court, and likely laid open the old wounds inflicted by his troubles with his own barons and earls, and his near civil war. The Bruce returned the Shield and Privy Seal of England to him, which he accepted, no doubt graciously, but this must have stung a bit as well.

England had support of the papal offices and had convinced the Pope to excommunicate the whole country of Scotland. But by 1317 Pope John XXII had sent two cardinals to England to try and convince Edward to make truce with Scotland. Edward held his single-minded stance and refused. Peace did not seem to be an option for him.

8 THE DECLARATION OF ARBROATH

ROBERT THE BRUCE could not have known how important to the world's history his next action to free his own country would be.

In a response to the continued support the Pope was lending to England, and the excommunication of Scotland from the church, a document was drawn up. It is widely believed to have been composed, on behalf of the barons and earls, by Bernard de Linton, Abbot of Arbroath and Chancellor of Scotland. This document of declaration, with the seals of eight earls and 45 barons attached, along with two other letters from King Robert Bruce, was sent to the Pope at Avignon in France in April 1320, carried by Sir Adam Gordon.

Titled 'Letter of the Barons of Scotland to Pope John XXII', but better known as 'The Declaration of Arbroath', this is considered to be the most important and famous document in all of Scotland's history, with very good reason.

I was standing in my shop one day, about eight years ago, when a well-dressed man came in. As he looked around he spotted a tea towel hanging on the wall. It was printed with

Modern photo from a re-enactment of the Declaration of Arbroath
Image courtesy of the Stirling Smith Art Gallery and Museum

a nice and bright Celtic knotwork border and had the most famous and most quoted line from the Declaration of Arbroath on it:

> For so long as a hundred of us remain alive,
> we will never submit ourselves to English dominion.
> We fight not for glory nor riches nor honours;
> but only and alone we fight for freedom,
> which no good man gives up,
> but with his life.

At the bottom it's stated:

> Declaration of Arbroath 1320

He turned to me and said, 'What is that?'

I responded, 'That sir, is the first statement of democracy in the world.'

He said, 'No... that would be the Magna Carta.'

I smiled and said, 'I'd have to disagree. You see, the Magna Carta states that the monarchy must live by the same laws as the people that they mean to rule. That is still feudalism... serf and lord... you see, that was in England.

'But the Declaration of Arbroath of Scotland... drawn up by the barons and earls and Good King Robert the Bruce in the year 1320, states... we the people of Scotland have brought the great King Robert the Bruce to the throne of Scotland because he believes in and will uphold and defend the cultural beliefs and laws of the Scottish people. But if he's ever to side against us and aid our enemy... we'll oust him and get a new king! That's democracy! A king, not brought to the people by God... but by the people, and chosen from the people, to work for the people, and also to be disposed of by the people if things go wrong.

'This was the first time in history that these thoughts were put forth: the concept that the true gift from God is freedom, and that that gift supersedes all else. Scots are born free, you see... and that freedom should not be taken from them, either by other ruling kingdoms or by the church... this document was sent to the Pope.'

I paused to let him digest what I'd just said. He looked over the tea towel again. I continued...

'I guess the roots of this idea go way back to the days of the Gaelic clans and their chiefs. When people hear the word 'chief', they immediately think of Ruler with a capital 'R'. Their concept of the word 'chief' is based on a feudal mindset. When, in fact, it was not... the Celtic chiefs were considered to be the first among equals; they were chosen from the body of the clan for their ability and know-how, but if they were ever to move against their own, they were disposed of and a new chief was chosen... feudalism came much, much later. And I suppose the underlying concepts, from the olde days and olde ways, never really faded out completely.

'The king or queen in Scotland, unlike other countries, was always known as the King or Queen of 'Scots'... not the king or queen of 'Scotland'. Scotland has always been seen as belonging to the people... and not just the itinerant people of the day, but all the Scots, from all times... the past, present and future. I guess that's one of the reasons that there's no enforceable trespassing law in Scotland, even to this present day. The Scots still have the right to roam freely throughout Scotland. Just a differing approach to life, I suppose, that's rooted in ancient times, but not lost in the modern day.'

He then said, 'I'm a Professor of History, at X University, and I'm ashamed to say I've never heard of this before today.' (The name of the University has been deleted to protect the innocent.)

I took him over to the bookshelf and handed him a copy of *The Declaration of Arbroath* by James Adam[4], and said, 'Here... take this as a gift... and go teach others... that's what it's all about, eh?' Knowing that I didn't have the time, and doubting that he would have the energy, for me to tell him the background info that brought the declaration into existence, I left it at that... but found myself hoping as he left the shop in what could only be described as a mild state of shock, that this book and information would spark him to go on and

---

4 Herald Press, Abroath, 1993, reprinted 1995

learn more – about the Bruce, the Wallace and the Scottish Wars of Independence – and in turn, teach others.

Though the most well known lines from the declaration are the ones already quoted, the deeper importance of the content is actually quite different. Although that famous quote does help to get the blood up, other notable statements are made, which should be pointed out.

The assertion that this King Robert has come to the throne by the choice of the nation really brings in the idea of the sovereignty of the people... in other words, the people are the ruling body of the kingdom, or rather the nation. And the fact that this kingship will be stripped from him if he does wrong by or to the people makes him sound a lot like an elected official. That's a major shift from the old truth of 'kings being brought by God', whereby if you questioned the king, it was like doubting God.

Arthur Herman, in *How the Scots Invented the Modern World*,[5] states that George Buchanan brought forth the 'new ideas' of democracy in 1579, with his published work *The Law of Government among the Scots*. He makes this statement:

> In [*The Law of Government*] Buchanan asserted that all political authority ultimately belonged to the people, who came together to elect someone, whether a king or a body of magistrates, to manage their affairs. The people were always more powerful than the rulers they created; they were free to remove them at will. 'The people' he explained, 'have the right to confer the royal authority upon whomever they wish.' This is the sort of view we are used to ascribing to John Locke; in fact, it belongs to a Presbyterian Scot from Stirlingshire writing more than a hundred years earlier. And Buchanan went further. When the ruler or rulers failed to act in the people's interest, Buchanan wrote, then each and every citizen, even 'the lowest and meanest of men,' had the sacred right and duty to resist that tyrant, even to the point of killing him. (Chapter One, 'New Jerusalem')

We can see that these ideals actually came from, and were set

---

5 Three Rivers Press, New York, 2001

down in, a document that appeared much farther back in Scotland's history than either Buchanan or Locke. Let's take a look at the Declaration of Arbroath, of 6 April 1320. In my own very loose, modernised version, the 'letter' states:

> The Scots have produced many great persons that are well known to the world. We have been around, as a nation of people, for over twelve hundred years. We then became one with the Picts, and threw off all other invading forces, and have always lived in freedom; history has shown these facts. One hundred and thirteen kings have reigned here, in our lands, of our own blood, and we were among the first to come to the church, with St Andrew, the great Apostle and brother of Peter himself, as Patron for our nation of people.

It goes on:

> Bearing this all in mind, also know that we lived with this protection and in peace and quiet, until Edward 1, father to the Edward that reigns now in England, invaded us and carried out monstrosities on our people and the leaders of the church, sparing none in these outrages. These evil outrages were such that they could not be truly known to any... except those that experienced them themselves.

> Now, Good King Robert the Bruce has delivered us up from these unbelievable evils, and has set free his people. Though faced with much hardship and many dangers, toils and wearinesses, he did this all with joy in his heart. And we will defend him with our own lives and our consent, as our chosen king. He has brought about our salvation, and safeguarded our liberties.

> But, if he should ever side against us and aid our enemies, we will bring him down from his position as king and cast him out as a subverter to our rights and the rights of our nation, and choose another to be our king to defend our freedoms.

> For so long as a hundred of us remain alive, we will never submit ourselves to English dominion. We fight not for glory, nor for riches, nor for honours, but only and alone we fight for freedom, which no good man gives up without his life.

It continues:

> ... asking the Pope to urge England to halt these actions against

the nation of Scotland, and be satisfied with what they have. After all it was good enough for the seven kings that had come before, or maybe more, in England. Leave the Scots to Scotland and Scotland to the Scots... to live in peace, within their own boundaries, since we want little more, and now have done all we can to secure this.

It also says:

... don't let the English convince you that their troubles with their neighbours, are keeping them from joining in the fight for the Holy Land, for they are really only finding more profit with less effort in attacking smaller and (in appearance) weaker bordering countries. If you persist in listening to the English and ignoring these facts, then God alone will be who you answer to, for the slaughter and evils, that will come from it.

We are obedient servants of God and the church, and now cast our plea to God, in the faith that he will grant us the strength and valour needed, to overthrow our enemy.

So the Declaration of Arbroath was signed and sealed, and sent to the Pope.

And that is why National Tartan Day in the United States is on 6 April each year. This national date was passed not only to honour the Scots in their fight for the freedom of their homeland, but to note the great impact that Scotland, its people and its history have had on the formation of the USA.

9 THE DE SOULES CONSPIRACY

ACCORDING TO A book by Peter Reese, *Bannockburn*,[6] some of the signatories of the declaration were really reluctant to be a part of it. This is demonstrated by the fact that their names do not appear in the main text, but are added only at the finish of it.

De Mowbray, Olifant and William Mowat were outspoken, and known to be supporters of the Balliol and Comyn families (according to Barbour, a noted Bruce biographer, and others). They went on to plot to kill Robert the Bruce, in what is referred to as the de Soules (or de Soulis) Conspiracy, after William de Soules, who was also a signatory of the declaration. De Soules was grandson to Alexander Comyn, Earl of Buchan, and was hereditary Senschal (or Butler) of Scotland.

The details of the conspiracy are unclear. Of the men involved, Brechin, Malhube, Logie and Squire Richard Brown were all condemned to death by a parliament held in Scone on 4 August 1320. Malhube, Logie and Brown were drawn, hanged and beheaded. De Mowbray died before he was convicted; his body was brought in front of the judges to be quartered, but the Bruce intervened and de Mowbray was spared this and given a decent burial. De Soules was condemned to perpetual imprisonment and confined at Dunbarton Castle, where it is said he died in a tower of stone. The same sentence was given to the Countess of Strathern, widow of the Earl of Malise and a supporter of the Comyns.

Following the conspiracy, King Robert distributed most of the traitors' lands among his loyal followers. Amongst these lands was the village of Gilmerton, just south of Edinburgh. Gilmerton was a possession of William de Soules and it passed to Murdoch Menteith.

Gilmerton was always known for its coal and limestone quarries – reputed to be the oldest in Scotland. But more intriguing are the dark secrets that the village holds out of

---

[6] Canongate, Edinburgh, 2000

sight, under the surface of its obvious history. Beneath the streets and shops of the village is a whole other structural world, which goes unnoticed by those bustling through their days above. 'Gilmerton Cove', as it is known, leaves scholars and investigators with more questions about its past than answers.

The Cove is a network of cavernous hollows carved from the sandstone below the village, creating a dwelling much like a house. Common history states that the Cove was single-handedly chiseled out by a local blacksmith named George Patterson in the 18th century. Completing his work in 1724, Patterson used this network of hollowed-out rooms and passages for his personal dwelling.

Within the twists and turns of the hollow are several apartments, a forge, beds, tables, and chairs, all carved right out of the sandstone itself. And each room cleverly receives its lighting from skylights above. In one of the rooms is what is referred to as a 'punch bowl', hollowed into the surface of a table.

It's recorded locally that Patterson was called before the Liberton Kirk (church) Session, charged with 'the serving of liquor inside his house on the Sabbath Day'. Patterson objected to these allegations and stated that he always pad-locked his home and carried the keys with him to kirk; that in fact it was his wife who had let drinkers into the dwelling through the back door.

His wife's reaction to this statement, unfortunately, is not recorded.

It is also said that the poet Pennycuik wrote the following inscription, which was carved into the stone above the fireplace:

Upon the earth thrives villainy and woe
But happiness and I do dwell below,
My hands hewn out this rock into a cell
Wherein from din of life I safely dwell.
On Jacob's pillow nightly lies my head,
My house when living and my grave when dead,
Inscribe upon it when I'm dead and gone
I lived and died within my mother's womb.

Pennycuik's poetic lines are not there now, but there is a sunken panel above the fireplace, and experts agree that a stone slab bearing his words could once have fit there very neatly.

F.R. Coles, Assistant Keeper of the Museum, Edinburgh, writing at the end of the 19th century, questioned the ability of one man to create this Cove by himself. He believed that the majority of the work had been done at least one full century earlier than when Patterson had lived. He pointed out that marks found on the stone by the creation of the subterranean hollows are from tools in use much earlier than Patterson's days.

Study of this unusual underground dwelling is still ongoing.

Much speculation has been raised as to its original purpose (before providing a residence for Patterson). It is said that the Knights Templar, the Masons, the Covenantors, smugglers, and strange cult-like groups may all have conducted meetings or ritual ceremonies there. (Carved markings on the surfaces resemble those associated with Masonic lodges, adding weight to this suggestion). It's thought that these secret societies and cults could have sought refuge in the Cove from the prying eyes of the common folk above ground. Or it may simply have been used for prostitution, drinking parties held by local gentry, or gambling.

With Gilmerton being in close proximity to the famous Rosslyn Chapel, there's even talk of the Holy Grail being buried somewhere in the reaches of the Cove. In one area excavation had to be stopped because of fears that the street above might collapse, so there is still more to be learned about this odd place.

We may never know exactly what the true purpose of the Cove was, but it is open to the public to visit, so you can come up with your own theory. It was on William de Soules's land, so who knows, maybe the de Soules Conspiracy got its start in the recesses of this underground hovel.

10 THE BLACK DOUGLAS AND THE BRUCE'S HEART

NOW COMES THE time to tell a tale that has been repeated for centuries. It is often told as a postscript or eulogy to the life of Robert the Bruce. It's a great testimonial to the trust and loyalty that he had achieved with his band of war companions... those that had stayed by his side, in council, in battle, in times of victory or defeat; through the times when Bruce entertained them with stories, and in times of complete despair; and now, in the time that he spent on his death bed and spoke of his last request.

He spoke to them of a vow he had made years before, that some day when the freedom of Scotland had been achieved, he would go to the Holy Land and fight in one of the Crusades. Now his homelands were free, and he had not the strength left to do this. The only thing left outstanding in his life was this vow he had made, and he still wished it to be honoured. He knew he was dying and that his time was to be soon. He told them that after he had passed, he wanted his heart to be removed, so it could be carried to the Holy Land to be blessed, and then returned to Melrose and the abbey there. He had thought this out carefully, and there was only one detail left... 'who will carry out the request for me?'

In immediate response, all his men, without hesitation, shouted, 'the Douglas'. James, The Black Douglas, tears filling his eyes, knelt down beside his dying friend and king and agreed to this last request.

It's said that when this Good King died the tears flowed freely like rivers throughout Scotland. Lament for his death knew no bounds of class, income or status, for he was loved by all. He passed away on 7 June 1329, one month shy of being 55 years old.

The Bruce's heart was removed and placed in a lead casket. The Black Douglas set out to fulfill the last request of his friend, taking with him a hardened band of fighting men. He carried the heart of the Bruce strung around his neck. But during the trek to the Holy Land, the Douglas and his men were caught up in a battle against the Moorish troops in

Spain and the Douglas was mortally wounded. Some say his last act was to throw the heart of the Bruce at the enemy, crying out, 'Go forward Brave Heart, and I will follow or die!' Others say that when the Douglas was found lying on the battlefield after the mayhem was over, the casket with Bruce's heart was lying beneath him.

It's a sad ending to a great story.

Here we have the most trusted friend and war companion of the Bruce, who had dedicated his life, long before, to the cause of Scotland and his king. The slightest mention of his name would strike fear in those that might chance to encounter him; when yelled out it could make the enemy turn to flee for fear of him: 'The Douglas! The Douglas!' It's said he had survived all those battles for his country without a scar left on his face. He'd gone on one last mission to honour an old friend, and came to this end.

His flesh was removed from his bones, and his heart removed from the flesh. It was carried by his men, alongside the heart of the great king, to Scotland and home. A last journey for two of the most noble and strong hearts to beat within the shores of Scotland. They still beat now in these stories... which today are told all over the world.

The Bruce's heart is buried at Melrose Abbey.

For more information on the life of Robert the Bruce and the Douglas, look for the books *James the Good: The Black Douglas*, and *On the Trail of Robert the Bruce* by David R. Ross.[7]

Following Bannockburn and the Declaration of Arbroath, nearly 400 years of self rule and freedom were enjoyed by the Scots... but those times were not always peaceful...

---

[7] Luath Press, Edinburgh, 1999 and 2008

UK

POLITICS, RELIGION AND THE JACOBITES

11 THE RISE OF THE JACOBITES

THE ROMAN CATHOLIC Church was under much scrutiny throughout Western Europe from the 16th century onwards. When Henry VIII of England was denied a divorce by the Pope, the king broke away from Catholicism and founded the Church of England, led by himself, through the Act of Royal Supremacy in 1534. In 1517 in Germany, Martin Luther was vocal against many of the doctrines held by the Catholic Church. Lutheranism and other Protestant beliefs gained strength, driving a political and religious wedge into societies across Europe, beginning the period of The Reformation.

The mid-1500s saw a major struggle between Scotland and England and the leading churches. The Catholic Mary Queen of Scots imprisonment and execution were ordered by Protestant Elizabeth I, Mary's cousin.

James VI came to the throne of Scotland in 1567. In 1603, with the death of Elizabeth I, he saw in the Union of the Crowns, becoming the first monarch to reign over both Scotland and England, as James VI and I.

By 1625 Charles I was monarch of the United Kingdom, but he lost the throne and his head to the Commonwealth and Cromwell in 1649. His son, Charles II, reclaimed the throne in 1660. Then in 1689, on 4 April, the parliament declared James VII of Scotland and II of Britain to be in forfeit of his crowns. William of Orange had landed in England the year before. He was married to James's daughter, Mary, and had been placed in charge. William and Mary were Protestants.

James VII and II, along with his infant son, escaped to France in a forced exile. This gave birth to the Jacobite movement (meaning supporter of James). The Jacobites were supporters of the 'rightful kings', the Stuarts, James VII and II, and his son and heir, also James. The Highland clans, led by John Graham of Claverhouse, Viscount of Dundee (known as 'Bonnie Dundee'), raised James VII and II's standard on Dundee Law. They met the government army and defeated them at the Battle of Killiecrankie, near Pitlochry. But the victory was dampened by the death of John Graham.

The Massacre of Glencoe

The massacre of the MacDonalds of Glencoe, on 13 February 1692, is considered to be one of the most tragic events in Scotland's history.

The Chief of Glencoe, Alasdair MacIain, had descended from the son of Angus Og of Islay, Iain (John) Og Fhraoich ('*fhraoich*' meaning 'heather' in Gaelic). He was also known as Iain Abrach (or 'Lochaber', after the area where he was fostered). Angus Og was with the Bruce at Bannockburn, and after the battle the Bruce gave the lands of Durrour and Glencoe and the isles of Mull and Tiree to him. Angus Og gave these in turn to his son, Iain Abrach. Iain Abrach died in 1358 and was buried on Iona, near his father. Eight Johns followed Iain in the line of descent. The MacDonalds of Glencoe, having no charter of their own, were included in the charters of John of Islay. After the forfeiture of the Lordship of the Isles in 1493, the MacDonalds became vassals of the Stuarts of Appin and the Campbells of Argyll. They joined Bonnie Dundee during the first Jacobite Rising to aid the return of their 'rightful king', James Stuart (though oddly the MacDonalds of Glencoe were not Catholics, but Protestant and Episcopal).

The Highland clan chiefs were told by the agents of William of Orange that they would receive full pardon for their actions in the Rising if they would sign an oath of allegiance to the king, no later than 1 January 1692. Refusal to sign would be met with the death penalty, not leaving a lot of room for choice.

Alasdair MacIain waited until the last minute to sign the

oath. He was waiting for word from James VII and II giving him permission to sign, to protect himself and his clanspeople and avoid the wrath of William of Orange and his troops. Some other clan chiefs had already received such permission and had taken the oath.

Word from James arrived on 29 December 1691, and MacIain set out for Fort William, reaching it on 31 December. When he arrived he found he must proceed to Inveraray, where he could take oath in the presence of a sheriff. It was approaching midnight, and MacIain couldn't believe he had to make a 60 mile journey through miserable, snowy weather. He had no idea what to think at this point... the man at Fort William, Hill, had taken oaths from others, but said the most he could give now was a letter of protection allowing MacIain to travel on. Hill insisted that the circumstances were different and he must go forward to Inveraray. MacIain knew that even in good weather, it was impossible for him to arrive on time. But he had no choice. He stayed in Fort William just long enough to get a letter of safe passage from Hill, then began the onward journey.

Along the way, MacIain and his gillie were arrested and detained further. This delay put them five days past the deadline by the time they finally reached their destination. After much deliberation with the Sheriff of Argyll (Campbell of Ardkinglas), MacIain took the oath on 6 January 1692 and went home, believing himself and his clan to be safe.

The Viscount of Stair, John Dalrymple, however, considered MacIain's oath to be invalid. He plotted, with others, one of them being the Duke and 10th Earl of Argyll, Archibald Campbell, to make an example of MacIain and his clan. On 1 February a company of soldiers arrived in the Glencoe area, to the alarm of the clan. They were assured that the troops were there temporarily and needed somewhere to stay for two weeks. MacIain pointedly asked the men of their intentions, and was told that they had billeting orders, commanding the clan to house and feed them, because there was no room in the Fort of Inverlochy (Fort William). In addition, the MacIains of Glencoe owed taxes, which they were there to collect. The three officers in charge assured MacIain that they had come with no hostile intentions. The Clan Chief Alasdair MacIain, against the advice of his sons and men, decided that the clan would be safe in allowing these men to stay, and would be protected under the standard code of Highland hospitality.

Now, that code was a point of honour and cultural law in the Highlands... even if someone came to your door with your death warrant, if you took them in and cared for them then they could and would do you no harm. The code had held true for centuries.

Besides, the man leading the troops was Robert Campbell, the uncle to Alasdair's own wife. So the MacDonalds took the unlikely guests into their homes, shared their winter stores of food and drink, swapped story and song, gambled with them, partied with them and treated them as the guests that they were supposed to be.

On 13 February at 5 am, with orders received, these same guests began to carry out a massacre of their hosts. Their orders were:

> Sir,
>
> You are hereby ordered to fall upon the rebels the MacDonalds of Glencoe, and put all to the sword under [the age of] 70. You are to have especial care that the Old Fox and his sons do upon no account escape your hands; you are to secure all avenues that no man escape; This you are to put in execution at five o clock in the morning precisely,
>
> Robert Duncanson

The idea was to kill all, so no man, woman or child would live to tell the tale. But things rarely work out the way they are planned. Of the 300 souls that lived in Glencoe, 38 died that night. MacIain and his wife were among those.

A knock came at MacIain's door at 5 am. It is reported that as the chief climbed out of his bed to put on his kilt, he called out for food and drink to be brought for his guests. He was cut down by a shot to his back. His wife was grabbed as she started to run for the door and she was stabbed repeatedly.

It is said that the soldiers bit the rings off her fingers in order to steal them. They left her for dead, and continued their carnage in other homes. She tried to escape through the hills with her son, but died from her wounds en route.

This incident has been considered the most dishonourable and treacherous act in the history of Scotland. Public outcry was enormous and could be heard throughout Europe. After all, if such a slaughter could happen in Glencoe, it could happen to any clan, or any town for that matter.

A commission was formed to look into the incident.

The findings were: that it was a great wrong to ignore the oath that MacIain had taken and that the orders 'seemed to have had a malicious design against Glencoe'; that John Dalrymple, Earl of Stair, knew MacIain had taken the oath; and that Stair's letters were the only warrant for what the commission called 'Slaughter under Trust':

> There was no instruction [given to Stair] for this slaughter nor the manner of it.[8]

There is a monument in Glencoe, which was erected in 1883. Every 13 February, MacDonalds come to this site from around the world, in memory of those that lost their lives that day in 1692. The monument states:

THIS CROSS IS REVERENTLY ERECTED IN MEMORY OF MCIAIN [sic] CHIEF OF THE MACDONALDS OF GLENCOE

WHO FELL WITH HIS PEOPLE IN THE MASSACRE OF GLENCOE 13 FEB 1692

BY HIS DIRECT DESCENDANT ELLEN BURNS MACDONALD AUGUST 1883

THEIR MEMORY LIVETH FOR EVERMORE.

I was present for the memorial service in 2006. I was very humbled, and honoured when asked to lay the wreath for the Glencoe Heritage Trust at the monument that day.

---

[8] The information on the descendancy of the chief of Glencoe and the commission's report comes from *Glencoe: A Short History*, purchased at the Glencoe Museum years ago, with no details of publisher or writer.

Many people have tried to make the massacre out to be another of the events of the long-time rivalry between the Clan Campbell and the Clan Donald (MacDonalds), but numerous clan names appear on the rolls of the soldiers that were there that night. And it's necessary to remember that those men were soldiers, and carrying out orders, under the threat of their own death.

Many years later, in 1745, Bonnie Prince Charlie was with his rebel army of Jacobites in Kirkliston, ready to march to Edinburgh. The prince was concerned that the Earl of Stair, a descendant of the Viscount of Stair, who lived nearby, might be harmed by those in the prince's ranks from Glencoe, the MacIains. A proposal was made to the MacIains that they should march a distance from Stair's residence, so that no harm would come to him for 'ancient wrongs'. The MacIains were deeply insulted by this and stated, 'if they were considered so dishonourable, that they would take revenge upon an innocent man... then... they were not fit to be with honourable men, nor to support an honourable cause.' The MacIains prepared to leave the prince's army for home, which would result in a great loss of strength to Bonnie Charlie and his army.

It was only through much persuasion that the MacIains were convinced not to leave, and to overlook what they considered to be a horrible insult. They stayed... but insisted that 'they alone' should guard Stair's residence, 'so no harm could befall him, and the men of Glencoe be blamed for it.'

William of Orange died in 1702, from a fall from his horse, which is said to have stepped into a molehill and thrown its rider. This accident was good fortune for the Jacobites, and gave rise to the drinking toast to 'the little gentleman in the black velvet coat', in reference to the mole.

William's wife, Mary, had passed on earlier, in 1694, so the crown passed to Anne, daughter of the deposed James VII and II, and Mary's sister, on 8 March 1702.

Because neither Mary nor Anne had had any children born

to them, the only successors to the throne on Anne's death would be James Stuart and his son, Charles (known as Bonnie Prince Charlie). The English leaders were having none of that (with the Stuarts being Catholic) and proceeded to pass legislation stating that upon the death of Anne the crown would pass to the House of Hanover. The Scottish parliament refused to recognise this ruling as valid, not wishing the English to choose the monarch for Scotland. The English, feeling quite threatened by this attitude, took measures against Scotland, restricting trade in all ways possible. This action damaged the economy in Scotland and set the stage for what was to follow.

12 THE ACT OF UNION 1707

THE MASSACRE OF Glencoe was just one of the incidents which led up to the Jacobite rebellions to come. The pinnacle event was the Union of the Parliaments.

Many will say, even today, that the Act of Parliament came to pass in 1707 solely because of the ill-fated Darien Scheme, but there were many other contributing factors... this was just the straw that broke the camel's back.

The Scottish East India Company, or Darien Company, came into existence by way of an Act passed by the Scottish parliament in 1695. This Act called for the establishment of a 'Company of Scotland Trading to Africa and the Indies', in an effort to create an outlet for products from Scotland, and later to settle a Scottish colony in Central America. This was, for the most part, funded by the merchants of Edinburgh. A man named William Patterson (who claimed to have founded the Bank of England) ultimately chose Darien, at the Isthmus of Panama, as the site for the colony, because of its ideal location as a hub for trade routes.

The project was hit by many complications: loss of settlers to severe illness; loss of ships... and the English moved against the Scots as competitors. This came to a boil when the English seized a Scottish ship in the Thames and the Scots countered by seizing an English ship, the *Worcester*, at Leith. Captain Thomas Green and the crew of the *Worcester* were arrested and charged with piracy; the captain, his gunner and his mate were all executed.

The Darien Scheme and all its troubles were only put to rest when the Act of Union was passed. The Act very conveniently included legislation to repay all the investors' money, with interest. This is what the great Bard of Scotland, Robert Burns, referred to as 'bought and sold for English gold' in his 1791 song 'Such a Parcel of Rogues in a Nation'.

The Act of Union legislation is, no doubt, one of the most debated pieces of history of the last 300 years. The date marking the 300th anniversary of its ratification was in January 2007, so it is very much on the minds and tongues of those in Scotland today. It supposedly brought the parliaments of Scotland and England together, but in essence it removed the Scottish parliament completely and moved the legislative power down below the border, to Westminster.

Many of the original 25 articles of the Act have been repealed or altered down through the years, and the Scots have felt the sting of it. The most well known of these alterations was the Community Charge, known as the Poll Tax of 1989, which went against Article XVIII (stating that taxes in Scotland and England would be the same). In 1989 the Poll Tax introduced a taxation on the Scottish people that was not imposed on the English, against this Article, and many in Scotland refused to pay it.

The Act of Union was welcomed by most of the English, and by others who would benefit from it (like those merchants that had so heavily invested into the Darien Project). But on investigation into the history of the Act you will see time and time again that 'there were riots on the streets in Scotland' and that 'only one in one hundred Scots agreed with it', and you will find the testimony of learned men stating what could and would go wrong in Scotland's future because of it.

A point of interest: John Dalrymple, former Viscount, now Earl of Stair, was heavily involved in the Act of Union... the same man that had been so heavily involved in the Massacre of Glencoe.

On 11 September 1997 (the 700th anniversary, to the day, of William Wallace's historic victory at Stirling Bridge) a vote was overwhelmingly passed, by 74 per cent, to bring back a Scottish parliament. The parliament has since reconvened, and is housed in a new building at Holyrood, at the bottom of the Royal Mile in Edinburgh.

13 THE KING ACROSS THE WATER

In 1708, James Francis Edward Stuart, later to be known as 'the Old Pretender', at the young age of 19, set out to claim his throne. Leaving Dunkirk with a small fleet of French ships and troops, he made his way to Scotland. They were to enter the Firth of Forth and disembark at Burntisland, then travel on to Stirling. But his plans were cut short by Admiral Byng of the Royal Navy and a squadron of English ships, who chased the French fleet around the northern part of Scotland. Though James pleaded to be put ashore, his request was not met. The ships returned to Dunkirk, ending his first attempt to bring the Stuart line back home to Scotland.

In 1714 Queen Anne died, and George 1 of the House of Hanover was placed on the throne of England and given the crowns of Scotland and Ireland. This event was not met with much joy by those in Scotland who still held the belief that the Stuarts were the rightful holders of the crown. The coronation, like the Union of the Parliaments, added to the unrest of Jacobites on both sides of the border, and in Ireland as well.

The Battle of Sheriffmuir

On 6 September 1715, John, the 6th Earl of Mar, raised the standard of James Stuart at Braemar. He'd already travelled to England to gather support, and by the month's end had approximately 12,000 men. He took occupation of Inverness, and held lands east and south to Perth by November. He then laid plans to invade England.

Word reached James Stuart, who returned to Dunkirk and (in disguise this time) set sail for Scotland.

At the same time, the 2nd Duke of Argyll, also John, gathered supporters of King George, about 4,000 men, and made way for the Firth of Forth, to block Mar's movement south.

Mar meanwhile had sent W. MacKintosh of Borlum and 2,000 men to join the Jacobites from the south west of Scotland in Edinburgh, which cut his forces somewhat, but their numbers still outranked those of Argyll.

They met at Sheriffmuir, north east of Dunblane, on the

slopes of the Ochils. The Hanoverians laid out their ranks on the high ground, with Argyll on the right and General Whetham on the left. The rebel army had MacDonnell of Glengarry, the Maclean of Duart and the MacDonald of Clanranald at centre and right. They struck hard and fast at the king's men and the left flank of the Hanoverian force was split immediately. Whetham fled to Stirling, where he announced his army slaughtered and defeated. But Argyll had attacked the rebels' other flank, where Mar was leading, and had pushed them back two miles. With the left flank of each army dead or scattered, both sides withdrew. They each claimed victory in this Battle of Sheriffmuir.

The failure to defeat the Hanoverians at Sheriffmuir resulted in the French and Spanish pulling their support for the Jacobite cause. James Stuart did not arrive in Scotland until the battle was already over. There was little he could do to rekindle the rebellion at this time.

The Battle of Glenshiel

The uprising of 1719 is commonly called the 'little rebellion'. The Spanish were heavily involved this time, for their own political reasons. A crafty plan was laid to unseat George I; a two-pronged attack would be made, to confuse and split the British military forces. The 10th Earl Marischal and the Jacobite forces from the Western Highlands and Islands, with 300 Spanish troops, would create a diversion in the north of Scotland to draw the British troops to them. Then the main Spanish force and their fleet would enter the south west of England, lay siege to London, depose George I and install James Stuart as king.

Things did not go as planned. The Spanish fleet was met with a damaging storm that thwarted their attempt to make the designated landing. The news of this turn of events spread through Scotland, hampering efforts to muster troops from the Highland clans for the other phase of the attack.

Eilean Donan Castle was made into a garrison for the ammunitions and supplies of the Jacobites' northern troops, and the Spanish were left to guard it while the Jacobites made their way to Glenshiel, en route to Inverness. The British government forces were well aware of these activities and sent an army out. The British and Jacobite forces met at Glenshiel on 10 June.

On the Jacobite side there were 200 Spaniards; Clan Cameron of Lochiel; Clan MacGregor, led by Rob Roy; Clan MacKinnon; the Seaforth MacKenzies, under MacKenzie of Coul and Lord Seaforth, chief of the clan and son of the chief of the Clan Murray; Clan MacKintosh of Borlum; and Clan Keith, led by the Earl Marischal; they comprised approximately 1,000 men. The British army had Clan Fraser, Clan Sutherland, Clan MacKay of Strathnaver, Clan Munro of Culcairn and others, making up close to the same numbers.

The battle only lasted around three hours before surrender was made by the Jacobites. The Highlanders disappeared into the mists to avoid capture and made their way home.

James returned to Spain, then went on to Rome to seek support from the Pope. Finding it, he settled there. He married the 15-year-old Clementina Sobieski, the granddaughter of the King of Poland, in that same year, 1719. Their union brought the birth of a son in 1720, Prince Charles Edward Stuart, 'the Young Pretender'... better known by his more affectionate nickname, 'Bonnie Prince Charlie'.

The Rising of the '45

The recently appointed Cardinal de Tencin was to help guide the policy of France. Tencin was a friend to the Stuarts, and was grateful to James for helping him with much of his advancement to his new post. He invited Prince Charles to come to France.

Charles held the same beliefs about being the 'rightful king' as his father, and had been brought up in a royal court in exile. He was keen to return the crown to the family line, and said to his father before leaving for France, 'I go, sir, in search of three crowns, which I doubt not but to have the honour and happiness of laying at your Majesty's feet.' James appointed his son as Prince Regent.

When the prince left Rome he had to do so in secret, as

Charles Edward Stuart (Bonnie Prince Charlie) painted from life, in Rome 1746
Image courtesy of the Stirling Smith Art Gallery and Museum

there were many spies from England about, who watched his every move and kept a close eye on his father and all those close to him. So a boar hunting party was planned, to cloak his departure to France. At an opportune time the prince rode off on his own, undetected. The party returned to Rome with gifts from the hunt, and someone dressed as Prince Charles rode through the countryside. The double was seen by many, so there was no suspicion of his absence.

The prince travelled in disguise, and reached Paris by 29 January 1744.

A plan was laid for a new invasion, but it was met with disaster in the form of another great gale. This storm dashed the hopes of the campaign by causing the destruction of many ships and the loss of lives. The English may at the time have believed that this was the end of the Jacobites and the Stuarts' bid for the throne, but the young Prince Charles had not given up hope. He said defiantly that he would return to Scotland the following year, 'though with but a single footman'.

1745 is commonly known as 'the Year of the Prince' through the lands of the Gaels.

The prince made preparations for the next campaign for the crown without discussing it with his father. Once on board ship and on his way, he wrote to James:

> I am to tell you what will be a big surprise to you. I have been, above six months ago invited by our friends to go to Scotland and carry what arms and money I could conveniently get; this being they are fully persuaded, the only way of restoring you to the crown, and them to their liberties... Your Majesty cannot disapprove a son's following the example of his father. You yourself did the like in 1715.

The letter was dated 7 March 1745.

So Prince Charles set off with the 'Seven Men of Moidart' in the ship called *Du Teillay*, accompanied by *The Elizabeth*. En route, *The Elizabeth* was attacked by the British ship *The Lion*, and the fight went on for at least four hours. Charles wanted the *Du Teillay* to aid *The Elizabeth*, but the captain refused to engage and *The Elizabeth* was forced to return to port because of damage sustained during the battle. The men with Charles tried to convince him to return as well, but he insisted on pushing on to their destination.

So on he sailed, with his seven men, in their single ship, to Scotland. On 3 August they made land on Eriskay, an island off the lower tip of South Uist, in the Outer Hebrides.

Imagine how he must have felt stepping onto the shore there, in the land where his grandfather had been king, and his father had attempted to regain the crown. Now it was up to him, the last of the Stuarts, and Prince Regent of the ancient line of kings that dated back to Robert the Bruce, and beyond. He was back in the home of all those before him, and ready to fight for what was rightfully his.

But the reality was that he had much work to do to meet his dreams. First he must add to his small rank of seven men by rallying the Jacobites to the cause. He would find out soon enough that not all felt as enthused as he did in this venture. He'd lost his small force of French troops with the return of *The Elizabeth*, along with a good portion of the arms that he had secured. This would be in the forefront of the minds of those he asked to come forward and help: the Highland chiefs.

The Prince was made aware of this early on, when Alexander MacDonald, on seeing that he'd no army to support him, told him to 'go home'. The Prince is said to have remarked, 'I am come home, sir...' He obviously had no intention of going back.

He raised his standard at Glenfinnan on 19 August. By September, he and those that came to his call had taken Edinburgh and won the Battle of Prestonpans.

Then, against the advice of his secretary, John Murray of Broughton, he invaded England, being persuaded by others in his ranks. Retreat from England followed on 5 December that year.

He had another victory at Falkirk, but was unsuccessful in trying to take Stirling, and headed north to Inverness. During this retreat, many of the Highland ranks disappeared, simply walking away to go home. The march into and retreat from England must have done more to convince them to leave than the victories won could do to convince them to stay.

The Battle of Culloden and the Aftermath

The Duke of Cumberland led the Hanoverian army to put an end, forever, to the Jacobite problem in the north. On 16 April 1746, Cumberland and his specially trained troops met the rebel army outside Inverness, at the field of Drummossie Muir, near Culloden. The location of the battlefield was just the first of the bad choices that led to this battle being a total loss for the Jacobites. Open field was not conducive to the way Highlanders fought, and there was confusion from the start.

Then the Highlanders were made to hold back while the Hanoverians shot cannonballs at them for an hour.

The Jacobites were itching to start the attack, but received no order to advance. When the clansmen were finally able to charge, Cumberland's men had a surprising technique waiting for them. Normally the Highland men would protect each other in their formation; the targe (shield) of one man helped to cover the man next to him from the blows of the enemy directly to his front. So Cumberland's men, for the first time in battle against the Scots, had been trained not to attack the man in front of them, but to turn slightly and attack the man to his side. This left that Highlander exposed to the thrust of their bayonet. This was another thing that led to the devastating defeat that day.

Cumberland was given the label 'the Butcher' following the actions of his men at Culloden, both during and after the battle. The wounded were shot or battered to death by the butts of rifles; even women and children were cut down. Clansmen were chased from the battlefield to be killed. Culloden turned from battle to vengeful carnage and the butchering of anyone that appeared to have been connected in any way to the rebel forces.

Prince Charles sent a note telling all those that had survived to scatter and find their way to their homes or other safe places. But he needed to find his own safe passage out of Scotland as well. There was a £30,000 price on his head, and 'Wanted' posters with his likeness on them were posted everywhere throughout the countryside. He spent many days and nights hiding from the Hanoverian ranks that were actively looking for him, and for anyone 'out with Charlie in the '45'. His salvation and freedom came to him from a very unlikely source, in the form of a Highland woman named Flora ('Fionnghal' in Gaelic) MacDonald.

Flora was born in 1722, the only daughter of Ranald MacDonald of South Uist, who died when she was two years old. Her widowed mother married Hugh MacDonald of Armadale, on the Sleat Peninsula, Isle of Skye, in 1728. Legend says that he abducted her and took her forcibly to his home, but regardless of how they ended up together, he is said to have been a good step-father to Flora and her brother Angus.

She was 24 years old when the Battle of Culloden took place. Her clan, the MacDonalds, were for the most part Jacobites, heavily involved in the battle, and afterwards they all felt the ramifications of it. All the clans that were 'out with Charlie' in the rebellion were looked upon with much suspicion, and government troops were blanketed all over the Highlands and Islands, looking for the prince.

Flora was approached by the prince and his men during the night. One of the men was Neill MacEachan, Flora's cousin and a secret agent for the French Service. They were trying to find a safe route for Charles to return to France. At first Flora did not want to be involved. The local people on the island feared the reprisals that would be brought against them if the prince was caught in their midst. But she finally agreed to help, since this would remove the prince from the village, and thus alleviate the danger to the people.

The prince was dressed as an Irish handmaiden and named Betty Burke. Neill was dressed as a servant. Flora was given a note of safe passage, listing her own name and those of these two characters, and they boarded a small boat to flee to the Isle of Skye.

The note of safe passage reads as follows:

My dear Marion
I have sent your daughter from this country lest she should be anyway frightened with the troops lying here. She has got one Betty Burke, an Irish girl, who, she tells me, is a good spinster. If her spinning please you, you can keep her till she spin all your lint or, if you have any wool to spin you may employ her for this purpose. I have sent Neil MacEachainn along with your daughter and Betty Burke to take care of them.
I am your dutiful husband
Hugh MacDonald.[9]

---

[9] *Prince Charlie and his Ladies* by Compton MacKenzie, New York, Alfred A. Knopp, 1935, p88.

The people of Skye aided the Prince in finding his way to France. He lived out his life as a broken man, steeped in alcoholism and self-pity. He was never able to get over the fact that he had failed in his attempt to regain the throne for his father, nor the cost of lives that had come from it. But the faith that the Highlanders had had in him and the high esteem they'd held for him were neverending, and many waited still for the 'king to come across the water' once more and return their liberties.

Flora spent time in the Tower of London for her part in bringing about the Prince's departure to safety, and became a folk hero. Her life took her to the American shores and Canada. Then, in her last years, she returned to Skye and was buried there. A memorial to her can be found in the north of Skye, in Kilmuir Cemetery, where she lies. The sheet that the prince slept on during his stay with her is said to have been used as a shroud for Flora's body.

The battle at Culloden brought about the final chapter in the history of the Highland clans. The system had been broken by the forfeiture of the Lordship of the Isles in 1493, and in the 1700s the fight to restore the 'rightful king' and remove 'foreigners' from the ruling power in Scotland destroyed it completely. In 1747 the Proscription Act was passed, which outlawed the wearing of the plaid (or tartan) and Highland dress in the Highlands and elsewhere, by anyone other than the Royal Military. This was an effort to break the backs of the clanspeople and their long-held tradition of dress and life. In order to be allowed to continue to wear the traditional dress of the Highlands, one would have to join the British military forces. This, combined with the regular pay, enticed many to serve. The Proscription Act was repealed in 1782, at the urging of a London Highland Society.

A mixture of politics and religion brought down a social system that had been in existence for centuries. But the ideals that came from that system are still held fast by those that live in the Highlands and Islands of Scotland today... and by those that have descended from the clans and spread all over the world.

After Culloden, many fled to the 'new world' of America and Canada. This saw the first large migration out of the Highlands. Many of these emigrants, and their descendants, were to play a part in what unfolded in their newly found home, and in the fight for freedom there.

There's a great story that encompasses some of the history we've covered here, 'The Curse of the Nine Diamonds'. I was told this when I was young, and it goes like this:

A long time ago, a man of the name George Campbell tried to steal the 'Treasures of Scotland' from Edinburgh Castle, where they were kept in security for all of Scotland. During this theft attempt, Campbell was interrupted, and he was only able to get away with nine diamonds.

The powers of the day sent many men to look for George Campbell, all over Scotland and beyond... but they could not find him. Because of this, and his being a 'common man', the powers thought that the people of Scotland might be helping him to hide, so they imposed a very heavy tax on the people to pay back the price of those 'nine diamonds'.

The people of Scotland were hurt economically by this added tax, and grew to dislike this man, George Campbell, and what he had done to them and their country. From that day forward, every time a Nine of Diamonds came up while playing cards it was called 'the George Campbell': the first part of the curse.

On the coat of arms of the Earl of Stair, John Dalrymple, the man that ordered the Massacre of Glencoe and was deeply involved in the Act of Union, by which Scotland lost her parliament and much of her legislative power, there are nine diamonds: the second part of the curse.

When the Butcher Cumberland had gleefully beaten the Jacobite army at Culloden, being a gambling man (it's said he laid bets with his men as to what the rebels would do next), he grabbed a playing card to write a note of his victory to the king, and that playing card just happened to be... you guessed it... the Nine of Diamonds: the third part of the curse.

Another version says that Cumberland picked up a playing card and wrote 'No Quarter' on it, to be sent to his commanders. 'No Quarter' meaning, 'spare none from death'. And that card was the Nine of Diamonds.

I've never confirmed the facts, but it's a good story... for everyone except George Campbell, I suppose.

USA

THE COLONISTS AND THE REVOLUTIONARY WAR

14 CALL FOR FREEDOM ACROSS THE GREAT WATERS

THE MIGRATION FROM Scotland to America started early on in the 1600s. Thousands of Scots were sent over to the colonies as prisoners, and sold into servitude as 'indentured servants'. This was often a seven year service, with release into freedom at the end of it, sometimes with pay and an award of lands. Other Scots came to the Americas by their own decision, looking for a more sustainable way of living, but even then many had to enter into servitude to pay for their passage to the New World. Each new event in Scottish history, whether it was the Jacobite rebellions or the failure of crops (eg. by 1775, over 100,000 Ulster Scots had crossed the waters), saw an increase in the flow of migration.

Many of the Ulster Scots were supporters of William of Orange and Protestantism. In Scotland these supporters were known as 'Orangemen' or 'Billy Boys'. They brought with them to the new land many of the stories and songs telling of the days of King William and his men. Soon the Ulster Scots who settled in America, in the Ozark and Appalacian Mountains, were to be known as 'hillbillies'.

For the Jacobites, the rebellions had failed to bring back the 'rightful king', and foreign domination of their country continued. Those that were involved in Culloden, and their relatives, were now considered criminals, or at least looked at with suspicion by the ruling Hanoverians. The choice to emigrate was not a hard one for many. Between 1760 and 1775 approximately 40,000 Scots left for North America and the colonies. Among them was Hugh Mercer, who had served as an assistant to the surgeon in the Jacobite army under Bonnie Prince Charlie. Mercer would later be killed by the English, while once again fighting tyranny at the Battle of Princeton in the American Revolutionary War. One of his descendants was General George Patton.

1760 also saw the third George of the Hanoverian line take the crown of England and Scotland, with ruling authority over the North American colonies. By 1764 the parliament in England started to pass legislative Acts imposing restrictive laws on the colonies, which were to lead to the first rebellion. The Sugar Act, which aimed to raise money from the colonies for the benefit of the British crown, introduced tariffs on non-British goods, giving British goods the economic edge in the marketplace, while the Currency Act prohibited the colonies from issuing their own currencies. These Acts were met with open protest and anger by the colonists. By the end of the year, the colonists had a full boycott of British goods in effect.

The Quartering Act was passed the next year, mandating the colonists to provide British troops with barracks and supplies. This was closely followed by the Stamp Act, introducing taxation on dice, playing cards, newspapers and pamphlets, almanacs and broadsheets (or broadsides – large sheets of paper with a vigorously written political message on one side, which were posted in public view or handed out). A tax on legal documents was also included in this Act. The 'stamp' referred to was produced in Britain and was applied to an item to show the tax had been paid.

In response to all this oppressive legislation, the colonists organised themselves. A network of secret organisations known as the 'Sons of Liberty' sprang up throughout the colonies. At first they concentrated on intimidating tax agents; it is said that all the agents had resigned before the British could implement the Stamp Act.

Stamp Act protest by William Bradford

The colonists drew up and issued a 'Declaration of Rights and Grievances', stating they were under oppressive action from the British government, with 'taxation without representation'. That is, they were being taxed by the parliament in England without having a representative there to speak for them. They felt that until the colonies had representation at Westminster they should not, by rights, be taxed, and refused to pay. The boycott of British imported goods continued.

Paying the Exciseman by Philip Dawe, 1774

In 1766 the Stamp Act was repealed and the ban on British imports stopped. But on the same day Westminster passed the Declaratory Act, which said Britain had the right to pass laws that were binding to the colonies 'in all cases whatsoever'.

New York was feeling the pinch of having so many British troops quartered there. Resistance to this rose, and the New Yorkers refused to allow their quarters to be used by the army. The reaction at Westminster was to strip the New York assembly of its power. Soon the assembly relented and gave money for the troops to the governing agents.

In 1767 the Townshend Act was passed, to pay for the 'increasing costs of governing the Colonies'. It taxed glass, lead, paper, paint and tea. Once again the colonists boycotted the purchase of British imports. In 1768 the Massachusetts legislative body was dissolved by the British government, in response to the statement about 'taxation without representation'. The call for all colonies to resist this was put out by Samuel Adams, and in 1769 Virginia experienced the same treatment.

In 1770 the Townshend Act was reduced by the British to only include taxation of tea. In response, the colonists once again eased the boycott campaign. There was conflict in New

Bostonians in Distress by Philip Dawe

York between the citizens and British troops after the Sons of Liberty's leader published a broadsheet attacking the New York assembly for complying with the Quartering Act. Riots took place, with injuries but no fatalities resulting.

In Boston there was public protest at the arrival of more British troops. On 5 March the troops surrounded the protesters and opened fire on them, killing three and seriously injuring others. The troops withdrew to an island in the harbour. The subsequent trial convicted the soldiers of much lesser charges than the murder that they had committed.

In 1772 a customs schooner, *The Gaspee*, grounded near Providence, Rhode Island, was attacked. The royal governor issued warrants for those involved but said the trial would be held in England. This brought more outrage from the colonists.

Samuel Adams called for a 'Committee of Correspondences' to communicate with other colonies on political matters. The other colonies followed suit and created their own committees.

In 1773 the Tea Act reduced the taxes on tea from Britain, giving British merchants the edge in the marketplace once again. This Act was condemned by the colonists, and the boycott came back into play. British tea already lay in the harbour onboard ships and the colonists wanted it shipped back to England, but the royal governor insisted the taxes must be paid in full and the tea unloaded for market.

On 16 December a group of men disguised as Mohawks boarded these ships, broke open the containers housing the tea and dumped it in the harbour waters. They took care to clean up after themselves, and even replaced a padlock they had broken. Their target was the tea and they wanted everyone to know it; nothing else was damaged or destroyed.

The Destruction of Tea at Boston Harbour, 1773, copy of lithograph by Sarony & Major 1846. This event has come down through history as the 'Boston Tea Party'

Of the men who carried out this protest, three are known to be from Scotland: Colonel John Murray of Perthshire, Colonel William Fleming of Lanarkshire and Captain John Swan of Fife. These men were members of the Masons, an organisation that had a very heavy influence on the ideals that guided the formation of the new country.

The British responded to the Boston Tea Party by passing more legislation to punish the colonists in Massachusetts. The Port Bill banned the loading and unloading of ships from the Boston harbour. The Administration of Justice Act protected royal officials in Massachusetts and allowed them to transfer cases against themselves back to England, such as revenue collection cases and the suppression of riotous acts by civilians. The Massachusetts Government Act virtually eliminated the charter of government in Massachusetts and allowed the election of governmental officers to be controlled by the Crown. And the Quartering Act was amended to allow the quartering of troops in 'any' occupied dwelling, which meant the colonists' own homes could now be taken over by the army.

Named delegates were organised from each colony, and they held the first Continental Congress in Philadelphia on 15 September 1774. Twelve of the 13 colonies were represented, Georgia being the only one that did not show. In all, 56 delegates were present. These delegates carried back to their home colonies the need to ban the purchasing of any British goods, and to set up committees to enforce this. New England made preparations to go to war. Militiamen rose up by the thousands

The Battle of Lexington, April 19 1775. Copy of print by John Baker 1882

among the colonists, making ready for actions of resistance and the coming of war. The 'Minute Men' formed and prepared for immediate response to military action.

The British responded by increasing troops and seizing ammunitions from Massachusetts, without incident. In 1775 the New England Restraining Act banned trade by the colonies with anyone other than Britain. Royal

Washington taking control of the American Army at Cambridge, Mass. July 1775, Currier and Ives, 1876. George Washington is named as commander-in-chief and a military draft commences, gathering troops for the Continental Army

authority pushed enforcement of the new Acts and made ready for the coming war. New England resisted. Troops tried to seize more of the ammunition in Massachusetts, but were turned away, again without incident.

The Committee of Safety in Boston learned of British movement to Concord, and in the dark of night sent out Paul Revere and William Dawes to raise the militia to meet the British forces there. The colonists' intelligence network was

Washington crossing the Delaware. artist E. Leutze, engraver J. Rogers

very good, and they were usually aware of British movements. Their opposition did not benefit from any such network, and had a hard time guessing what the 'Americans' would do next.

On 19 April 1775 the Minute Men met British troops at Lexington, where the 'shot heard round the world' was fired, and the war officially started.

The British went on to Concord to destroy an ammunition depot, but found the countryside swarming with militiamen (thanks to Paul Revere's 'midnight ride'). At the end of the day, many lives were lost on both sides.

On 10 May the Continental Congress met again. John Hancock was elected as president of congress and George Washington was appointed commander-in-chief. On 10 June John Adams named the patriot forces in Boston the 'Continental Army'. 12 June saw the Battle of Bunker Hill. The British General Gage issued the order of Martial Law and said anyone taking part or helping the rebel forces would be considered 'a Traitor and a Rebel themselves' and would be prosecuted. The British rejected the 'Olive Branch Petition' sent by the Continental Congress to find a reconciliation and avoid further conflict and hostilities. Four months later, George III declared the colonies in a state of rebellion.

The Revolutionaries were known as 'Patriots' or 'Americans', and made up about 40 per cent of the population. 15 to 20 per cent supported the Crown and King George III, and were known as 'Loyalists'. Over the eight years of war, a quarter of a million men and boys served in the 'Cause for Independence' as militia or Minute Men, with less than 100,000 serving at any given time.

Many of these men were of Scots and Irish birth or ancestry, and fought as they had in Scotland and Ireland. Others were unskilled in war tactics and more familiar with farming implements. Regardless, they had a heart for freedom and would fight to the ends of the earth to support their leader, George Washington, in their cause. Washington was obviously very aware of this, and made a statement that shows how important these men from Scotland and Ireland were to him and to the fight for independence. When he was at Valley Forge, in the harshest of winter weather, his men were starving and exhausted. The conditions were so bad that it's been said the men's feet were freezing to the ground while they rested. Washington wrote a letter and sent it by courier to another commander. It said:

> If all else fails, I will retreat up the valley of Virginia, plant my flag on the Blue Ridge, rally around the Scotch–Irish of that region and make my last stand for liberty amongst a people who will never submit to British tyranny whilst there is a man left to draw a trigger.

Now that's a pretty bold statement, and it harkens back to that one from the Declaration of Arbroath:

> For so long as a hundred of us remain alive, we will never submit ourselves to English dominion.

It shows that the century may have changed, but the ideals were not lost with the passing of time, and were carried forth with those Scots that came to America. They believed that they were born with certain 'rights in life' that could not be taken away by a governing body. In light of their having no representation with that governing body, they did not hold with the idea of taxes, restrictions of trade, restrictions of currency and the abolishment of their chartered assemblies of government, nor with the lack of 'due course of justice' for trials. All these were things that they felt they should not have to endure.

King George III was playing outside the realm of his 'documents of law', the Magna Carta, by removing rights from these people, if he actually considered them 'loyal subjects of the Crown'.

15 THE DECLARATION OF INDEPENDENCE

These are the times that try men's souls.

THOMAS PAINE

ALL OF THOSE involved in America's independence, whether they were leading in battle, fighting in the countryside as militia, drawing up documents in backrooms and taverns, or debating the issues in meeting halls, were at risk of wearing the hangman's noose, and few ever forgot it. They might have seen themselves as struggling for their freedom and for the formation of their

Benjamin Franklin said 'we must hang together, or surely we will all hang separately', referring to the need for a strong and united front.

'States', but in the eyes of the English they were carrying out acts of treason against the Crown and were no more than rebels.

'Common Sense' by Thomas Paine

Thomas Paine wrote with eloquence in his pamphlet 'Common Sense' about the absurdity of the idea of hereditary lines of kings, and how all men are equal and have their rights given to them by nature. Presented here are some of the passages from that influential text.

Paine starts his document, directly after his introduction, with a 'setting the stage' statement:

Thomas Paine by George Romney (1734–1802)

> SOME writers have so confounded society with government, as to leave little or no distinction between them; whereas they are not only different, but have different origins. Society is produced by our wants, and government by our wickedness; the former promotes our happiness POSITIVELY by uniting our affections, the latter NEGATIVELY by restraining our vices. The one encourages intercourse, the other creates distinctions. The first is a patron, the last a punisher.

And after setting the pace with the above words, he continues on with:

> Society in every state is a blessing, but Government, even in its best state, is but a necessary evil; in its worst state an intolerable one: for when we suffer, or are exposed to the same miseries BY A GOVERNMENT, which we might expect in a country WITHOUT A GOVERNMENT, our calamity is heightened by reflecting that we furnish the means by which we suffer.

The text clearly articulates his observations of the state of affairs in the colonies at the time and the oppression of the citizens at the hands of King George. Paine had no love for the system of hereditary kings or the avenue of abuse that this type of government had led mankind down, as the following lines show:

> To the evil of monarchy we have added that of hereditary succession; and as the first is a degradation and lessening of ourselves, so the second, claimed as a matter of right, is an insult and imposition on posterity. For all men being originally equals, no one by birth could have a right to set up his own family in perpetual preference to all others for ever, and tho' himself might deserve some decent degree of honours of his contemporaries, yet his descendants might be far too unworthy to inherit them. One of the strongest natural proofs of the folly of hereditary right in Kings, is that nature disapproves it, otherwise she would not so frequently turn it into ridicule, by giving mankind an ASS FOR A LION [the lion being a common symbol for a king].

> Secondly, as no man at first could possess any other public honours than were bestowed upon him, so the givers of those honours could have no power to give away the right of posterity, and though they might say 'We choose you for our head,' they could

not without manifest injustice to their children say 'that your children and your children's children shall reign over ours forever.' Because such an unwise, unjust, unnatural compact might (perhaps) in the next succession put them under the government of a rogue or a fool. Most wise men in their private sentiments have ever treated hereditary right with contempt; yet it is one of those evils which when once established is not easily removed: many submit from fear, others from superstition, and the more powerful part shares with the king the plunder of the rest.

Later, in reference to the actual system of government in place, he states:

Absolute governments, (tho' the disgrace of human nature) have this advantage with them, they are simple; if the people suffer, they know the head from which their suffering springs; know likewise the remedy; and are not bewildered by a variety of causes and cures. But the constitution of England is so exceedingly complex, that the nation may suffer for years together without being able to discover in which part the fault lies; some will say in one and some in another, and every political physician will advise a different medicine.

I know it is difficult to get over local or long standing prejudices, yet if we will suffer ourselves to examine the component parts of the English Constitution, we shall find them to be the base remains of two ancient tyrannies, compounded with some new Republican materials.

FIRST – The remains of Monarchical tyranny in the person of the King.

SECONDLY – The remains of Aristocratical tyranny in the persons of the Peers.

THIRDLY – The new Republican materials, in the persons of the Commons, on whose virtue depends the freedom of England.

The two first, by being hereditary, are independent of the People; wherefore in a CONSTITUTIONAL SENSE they contribute nothing towards the freedom of the State.

To say that the constitution of England is an UNION of three powers, reciprocally CHECKING each other, is farcical; either the words have no meaning, or they are flat contradictions.

FIRST – That the King it not to be trusted without being looked after; or in other words, that a thirst for absolute power is the natural disease of monarchy.

SECONDLY – That the Commons, by being appointed for that purpose, are either wiser or more worthy of confidence than the Crown.

But as the same constitution which gives the Commons a power to check the King by withholding the supplies, gives afterwards the King a power to check the Commons, by empowering him to reject their other bills; it again supposes that the King is wiser than those whom it has already supposed to be wiser than him. A mere absurdity!

Much later in his text these lines brings up the burning question:

But where says some is the King of America? I'll tell you Friend, he reigns above, and doth not make havoc of mankind like the Royal Brute of Britain. Yet that we may not appear to be defective even in earthly honours, let a day be solemnly set apart for proclaiming the charter; let it be brought forth placed on the divine law, the word of God; let a crown be placed thereon, by which the world may know, that so far as we approve of monarchy, that in America THE LAW IS KING. For as in absolute governments the King is law, so in free countries the law *ought* to be King; and there ought to be no other. But lest any ill use should afterwards arise, let the crown at the conclusion of the ceremony be demolished, and scattered among the people whose right it is.

A government of our own is our natural right: And when a man seriously reflects on the precariousness of human affairs, he will become convinced, that it is infinitely wiser and safer, to form a constitution of our own in a cool deliberate manner, while we have it in our power, than to trust such an interesting event to time and chance.

Paine finishes his text with the following:

To CONCLUDE, however strange it may appear to some, or however unwilling they may be to think so, matters not, but many strong and striking reasons may be given to show that nothing can settle our affairs so expeditiously as an open and determined declaration for independence. Some of which are,

FIRST – It is the custom of Nations, when any two are at war, for some other powers, not engaged in the quarrel, to step in as mediators, and bring about the preliminaries of a peace; But while America calls herself the subject of Great Britain, no power, however well disposed she may be, can offer her mediation. Wherefore, in our present state we may quarrel on for ever.

SECONDLY – It is unreasonable to suppose that France or Spain will give us any kind of assistance, if we mean only to make use of that assistance for the purpose of repairing the breach, and strengthening the connection between Britain and America; because, those powers would be sufferers by the consequences.

THIRDLY – While we profess ourselves the subjects of Britain, we must, in the eyes of foreign nations, be considered as Rebels. The precedent is somewhat dangerous to their peace, for men to be in arms under the name of subjects; we, on the spot, can solve the paradox; but to unite resistance and subjection requires an idea much too refined for common understanding.

FOURTHLY – Were a manifesto to be published, and despatched to foreign Courts, setting forth the miseries we have endured, and the peaceful methods which we have ineffectually used for redress; declaring at the same time that not being able longer to live happily or safely under the cruel disposition of the British Court, we had been driven to the necessity of breaking off all connections with her; at the same time, assuring all such Courts of our peaceable disposition towards them, and of our desire of entering into trade with them; such a memorial would produce more good effects to this Continent than if a ship were freighted with petitions to Britain.

Under our present denomination of British subjects, we can neither be received nor heard abroad; the custom of all Courts is against us, and will be so, until by an independence we take rank with other nations.

These proceedings may at first seem strange and difficult, but like all other steps which we have already passed over, will in a little time become familiar and agreeable; and until an independence is declared, the Continent will feel itself like a man who continues putting off some unpleasant business from day to day, yet knows it must be done, hates to set about it, wishes it over, and is continually haunted with the thoughts of its necessity.

'Common Sense' was produced in January 1776. Within its

The Committee of Five by Alonzo Chappel

pages, Paine tackled the same sort of problems that Scotland had experienced with the English and the 'Right of Kings' back in 1320. 'Common Sense' was considered the first call for independence by the Americans.

The 'Committee of Five' were selected from the body of the Continental Congress. They were John Adams, Benjamin Franklin, Thomas Jefferson, Robert Livingston and Roger Sherman. Their task was to draft a document of independence reflecting the sentiment put forth in Paine's pamphlet and encompassing the issues which existed between the colonial patriots and the British government. Not all those involved in the Congress were in total agreement with this action and document. Philip Livingston (New York) and John Dickinson (Pennsylvania) argued to delay the call for independence. No doubt their fears included failure in battle and the gallows.

But in July 1776, Richard Henry Lee presented the 'Lee Resolution', which read in part: 'That these United Colonies are, and of right ought to be, free and independent States, that they are absolved from all allegiance to the British Crown...' In this he was 'declaring Independence' for the United States. 'All political connections' between the US and Britain were to be 'totally dissolved'.

The Declaration of Independence was drafted and amended, corrections were made, language was softened or hardened where needed, and the final version was approved and sent to the printer on 4 July 1776.

The printer, John Dunlap, worked through the night, producing over 150 copies, which became known as the 'Dunlap

Broadsides'. Dunlap had been born in Strabane, Ireland in 1747. He was official printer to the Continental Congress. In 1787, he and his partner David Claypoole printed the Constitution of the United States and published it in their newspaper.

Then there was Benjamin Townes, who had started his own publishing house in 1774. By 1776 he was producing a newspaper called the *Pennsylvania Evening Post*, located in Front Street, near the London Coffee House. On 6 July 1776 he printed the Declaration of Independence on the front page, the first time it appeared in a newspaper. The *Pennsylvania Evening Post* was a tri-weekly newspaper, coming out on Tuesday, Thursday, and Saturday. Townes was a hard and fast supporter of the Americans' cause and his newspaper was one of the most widely read of the day. But Townes was to prove a bit of a turncoat and a definite opportunist. When the British occupied the city, he suddenly becomes a Tory, no doubt to save his own skin, as well as his business operation. Then, when the British pulled out of the city, he found himself the only printer still operating, and ended up with the contracts for the Continental Congress's printing needs.

Later, Townes became the first American to produce a 'daily' newspaper, in 1783.

John Baine, with Alexander Wilson, built the first 'Type Foundry', in St Andrews, Scotland, in 1741–42. Wilson was called 'The Father of Scottish Letter Founders'. Baine emigrated to Philadelphia and started the firm that was to produce the first type-set for the dollar sign in America.

George Washington received a copy of the Declaration of Independence while with his troops in New York and read it to them. Inspiration for the fight for freedom must have been extremely high at that moment, after the soldiers

The Declaration of Independence

Declaration of Independence by John Trumbull

heard the content of that 'end-all' statement for their independence from England. If they won, it would be the beginning of their own country; if they lost, it would be the death warrant for all involved.

Most of the colonial delegates had signed the declaration by 2 August 1776. The signing was done in the geographical order of the colonies, from the north to the south. Fifty-six delegates signed in all. The final engrossed copy is now displayed at the National Archives.

The Declaration

In Congress, 4 July 1776, the unanimous declaration of the 13 United States of America was made:

> When in the Course of human events, it becomes necessary for one people to dissolve the political bands which have connected them with another...

it begins, maintaining this direct tone till the end. Reading it, you'd think they had a 'no holds barred' approach, but they had actually softened the language in many places, at the urging of some of their members, so as to not commit political suicide in the worldwide arena. (Not all members of Congress were in agreement with the bid for 'total' independence. Fear of economic instability and reprisals from the British in the future were always in the forefront of their minds.)

> We hold these truths to be self-evident: that all men are created equal, that they are endowed by their Creator with certain unalienable Rights, that among these are Life, Liberty, and the Pursuit of Happiness.

'Rights' are given to men by their Creator and cannot be stripped away by kings, governments, or any other man. The Declaration of Arbroath too had stated this, long ago.

The Declaration of Independence goes on to say:

> [That] Governments are instituted among Men, deriving their just powers from the Consent of the Governed, that whenever any Form of Government becomes destructive of these ends, it is the Right of the People to alter or abolish it...

> Such has been the patient sufferance of these Colonies; and such is now the necessity which constrains them to alter their former Systems of Government. The history of the present King of Great Britain is a history of repeated injuries and usurpations, all having in direct object the establishment of an absolute Tyranny over these States.

It then lists all the offensive acts of the British that had been endured by the colonists, rounding up with:

> They too have been deaf to the Voice of Justice and of consanguinity. We must, therefore, acquiesce in the Necessity, which denounces our Separation, and hold them, as we hold the rest of Mankind, Enemies in War, in Peace Friends.

So we see another country of men announce their rights to the world, in their bid for freedom... and prevail in their effort.

Once the document had been signed by the delegates of the now United States of America, it was decided that a copy should be printed. Mary Katherine Goddard of Baltimore has gone down in the records as being the person who printed the first signed version of the historic document.

Thomas Jefferson by Thomas Sully. Thomas Jefferson is credited with penning the final draft of the Declaration of Independence.

The Signatories of the Declaration of Independence

Many who signed the Declaration of Independence had ancestral links to Scotland. Some carried names that originally hailed from Scotland; others had a more direct line. Other signatories came from Wales, England and Ireland. Here are some of them:

From Georgia: Button Gwinnett, born in Gloucestershire, England, 1735 of Welsh parentage.

North Carolina: William Hoopen, born to a Scottish Minister near Kelso. Attended Harvard at the tender age of 15.

South Carolina: Edward Rutledge, born Charleston, SC, 1749 to Dr John Rutledge, who had emigrated from Ulster in 1735. Rutledge is a small Border clan of Scotland; Thomas Lynch, Jr, of Irish/Dutch/English descent.

Maryland: Charles Carroll of Carrollton, Irish, and may have been the only Roman Catholic to sign the Declaration.

Virginia: Thomas Nelson, Jr, Scottish/English.

Pennsylvania: James Smith, Scot/Irish (this listing usually means Ulster Scot); George Taylor, Scot/Irish; James Wilson, born St Andrews, Scotland; George Ross, born of Scottish parents. His nephew, John Ross, was married to the now famous Betsy Ross, who handmade the first flag for America.

Delaware: George Read, Irish/Welsh; Thomas McKean, Scot/Irish. His great-grandfather was from Argyllshire in Scotland, and moved to Ulster in the 17th century.

New York: William Floyd, Welsh/English; Phillip Livingston, Dutch/Scottish; Francis Lewis, Welsh; Lewis Morris, listed as English/Dutch, but both his names can be found on the name rolls of Scotland.

New Jersey: John Witherspoon, Scottish.

New Hampshire: Mathew Thornton, Irish born, moved from North Ireland to America at the age of three.

Of the 13 governors to hold office in this newly found nation, nine were Scots. Archibald Bullock (Georgia), George Clinton (New York), William Livingston (New Jersey), John MacKinley (Delaware), Jonathan Trumbull (Connecticut), Richard Caswell (North Carolina), Patrick Henry (Virginia), Thomas McKean (Pennsylvania) and John Rutledge (South Carolina).

On 3 September 1783 the Second Treaty of Paris officially brought an end to the Revolutionary War. (The first Treaty of Paris had ended the Seven Years War.)

Key points were made in this Second Treaty:

- The recognition of the colonies as free and sovereign states.
- The establishment of borders, of the nation of states.
- Release of prisoners of war from both sides, without molestation.

On 14 January 1784 the Treaty was ratified by the Continental Congress. The British ratified it on 9 April, and an exchange of documents followed on 12 May, bringing to a close this long and complicated struggle for freedom and marking the formation of a new nation.

Adam Smith wrote in his famous *Wealth of Nations*:

> The persons who now govern the resolutions of what they call the Continental Congress, feel in themselves, at this moment, a degree of importance which, perhaps, the greatest subjects in Europe scarce feel. From shopkeepers, tradesmen, and attorneys, they are become statesmen and legislators, and are employed in contriving a new form of government for an extensive empire, which they flatter themselves will become ... one of the greatest and most formidable that ever was in the world.

Adam Smith left his mark on history not only in his native home of Scotland, but around the world. Many others that left their mark on this period of history came from Scotland, some by way of Ireland's northern region. The names of many of the fallen and unsung men and women from that realm may never be known, but I've found some interesting tidbits while researching this book.

Dr William Brown, born in Haddington, served as the Surgeon General for the Continental Army. He also produced the first book of pharmacopeia in America.

General Lachlan MacKintosh, born in the Kingussie area, became a very high-ranking commander of the revolutionary army in Georgia.

Alexander Hamilton, First Secretary of the Treasury, was a Scot.

Rev. John Witherspoon, a minister from Scotland, became the sixth president of the College of New Jersey, now known as Princeton University.

James Wilson wrote the legal observation that unless the Americans had representation in the British parliamentary procedure, the British government should have no authority over them. This idea of 'taxation without representation' became a driving force and a battlecry of the revolution. Wilson, as a lawyer, at first refused to sign the Declaration of Independence because of the conflict of interests arising from those he represented. When he did sign, it opened the floodgates for others to enter the arena, giving their own support for the freedom cause in Pennsylvania.

John Paul Jones, from Dumfries and Galloway, emigrated at the age of 12, and later founded the US Navy.

Alexander McDougall, born on Islay, ran the military academy at West Point.

Archie MacDonald, from Glencoe, was the first fur trader to travel to the West Coast of America and start up a trading post there, at the mouth of the great Columbia River. This post was then sold to the Hudson Bay Company and became the first settlement on the West Coast. It was called 'Astoria', named for John Jacob Astor. MacDonald's family traded with the Native Americans in other areas as well, one being Montana. His influence can still be seen there. There is a lake in Glacier National Park called MacDonald Lake, named for a Nez Perce Chief called MacDonald. Archie's offspring had married into the Nez Perce tribe and many now carry the name MacDonald. More can be read on this interesting bit of history in a book by James Hunter called *Glencoe and the Indians*.[10] I had the good fortune to meet one of the descendants of this family of Native Americans in a pub in Seaside, Oregon. It was a great experience. I had read Hunter's book only the year before, and a relative of the man I met had worked with Hunter during his research phase. Our conversation began

---

[10] Mainstream, Edinburgh, 1997

because we were both drinking the same whisky; then we found we had the same last name, MacDonald.

Abraham Lincoln had a son (reported to be his favourite) named William Wallace, who died while Lincoln was president and in residence at the White House.

Neil Armstrong, the first man on the moon, was born to a family from Langholm, Dumfriesshire.

The list can go on and on; the more you uncover, the more light is shed on just how much the Scots have influenced and impacted the formation and growth of the nation called America.

16 GEORGE WASHINGTON AND THE SNUFF BOX

IN SEPTEMBER 2005, I was at a conference on William Wallace at the Smith Art Gallery and Museum in Stirling. It was a day-long conference, commemorating the 700th anniversary of the execution (or murder, as some call it) of William Wallace by the English.

Dr Elspeth King, the curator, had invited me to come and represent the United States as a presenter that day, and speak on the influence that the life and legend of Wallace have had on America. Each person presenting covered an area in Scotland that was important in Wallace's life and actions. It was a brilliant conference, as is usual at the 'Smith', thanks to Dr King and her staff. During the day, one of the presenters spoke of the Torwood Wallace Oak and the history connected with it.

Now the Torwood was important in the life of Wallace, and within that wood stood a huge and ancient oak tree. It's said that the trunk had a 12-foot diameter, and the branches were thick and rich with foliage and spanned 80 feet or more. Wallace used this wood, once part of the great Caledonian Forest, to rally his men and take refuge. There are stories of Wallace and maybe two or three of his men sleeping inside the hollow of the trunk, and of him sleeping in the branches. The size of the tree was so vast, that it could hold and hide 40 men or more, and so on.

But there is one particular story that's heard more than the rest.

After the Battle of Falkirk and the terrible defeat of that day, Wallace escaped the battlefield but was pursued by Edward and his men. Wallace ducked into the forest and disappeared. While Edward frantically searched for him, Wallace watched on... from the safety of the branches of this mighty oak.

This is the story that is normally told when the subject of the Torwood Wallace Oak comes up.

On the day of the conference, the speaker told another story that I'd not heard before, about a snuff box that had been made from a chip of the wood from this mighty oak for the 11th Earl of Buchan in the late 1700s. The earl, in turn, gifted it to George Washington when he became the first President of the United States.

In the Spring of 2006, when I started to do research for this book, I thought this story would be nice to include, but the details of it had faded a bit. So I contacted Dr Elspeth King at the 'Smith' to see if she could help me recapture the information.

In the opening of her response she said:

> The story of the box is a long one. It was made from the ancient Wallace Oak in the Torwood, near Stirling, by the Edinburgh goldsmiths for David Stuart Erskine, Eleventh Earl of Buchan (1742–1829).

> The Earl of Buchan was a patriot and a radical who supported both the American and the French Revolutions, and he presented the box to George Washington, whom he considered to be 'the Wallace of America'. This was quite a daring thing to do; others were being deported for similar political beliefs, but Buchan was from one of the aristocratic families, and was not actively prosecuted.

She continued with more of the details. She also stated that she had searched for the box in 1996–7, for a Wallace exhibition she was working on for the 700th anniversary of the Battle of Stirling Bridge, 'all to no avail'. But there was a rumour that it had been donated to the Daughters of the American Revolution in 1923.

She closed saying:

> When I saw the open storage in the New York Historical Society's museum, and the riches it contains, it occurred to me that the box might well lie in such a collection in the USA, unnoticed somewhere. If you could raise some interest in it again and track it down, it would be wonderful. I'm going to attach two images to this message – one an engraving of the Wallace Oak in the 1770s, and another of about 1800, when just a stump of it remained. So many things were made out of it – sadly, we don't have any of them – and it would be great if you could find the box again.

The message came in by email early one morning. The

same afternoon, I got a gut feeling that I should go look for it. I opened my laptop, went to the internet, and typed in 'Daughters of the American Revolution'. The first listing on the first page was the DAR Museum site, so I clicked on it.

Wallace Oak, Torwood, circa 1770s, by permission of the Stirling Smith Art Gallery and Museum.

Then, to my total shock, the page said something to the effect of:

> Come see our new and unusual exhibit, we have just emptied our vaults onto the display floor. Come see all the strange and unique [or it could have said 'weird and wacky'] gifts that have been given to the US over the past 200 years.

My heart started to race. 'If they have it,' I thought. 'Now is the time to locate it, after all they've just emptied their vaults and catalogued the items.' So, I immediately sent off an email to Elspeth King, back in Scotland. I told her about the new information, and the 'Quest' for the location of the 'Wallace Snuff Box' was up and running.

Much to my joy, the DAR found, within weeks, a snuff box that fit the bill in a file drawer in their storage. They had had no idea that they had this item in their museum.

Wallace Oak, Torwood, circa 1800, by permission of the Stirling Smith Art Gallery and Museum.

Here's the story that unfolded:

The 11th Earl of Buchan, David Steuart Erskine, was a staunch supporter of the American Revolution, and deeply admired the actions and leadership of George Washington. He presented the Wallace Oak snuff box to George Washington when he came to the presidency, in 1789. Washington was very moved by the gift, and in his Last Will and Testament, left the snuff box to be returned to Buchan, so that a 'more worthy man' could be selected for it to be presented to.

> Item to the Earl of Buchan I recommit 'the box made of the Oak that sheltered the Great Sir William Wallace after the battle of Falkirk' presented to me by his Lordship, in terms too flattering for me to repeat, with a request 'to pass it, on the event of my decease, to the man in my country, who should appear to merit it best, upon the same conditions that have induced him to send it to me.' Whether easy, or not, to select the man who might comport with his Lordship's opinion in this respect, is not for me to say; but conceiving that no disposition of this valuable curiosity can be more eligible than the recommitment of it to his own Cabinet, agreeably to the original design of the Goldsmiths Company of Edenburgh, who presented it to him, and at his request, consented that it should be transferred to me; I do give and bequeath the same to his Lordship, and in case of his decease, to his heir with my grateful thanks for the distinguished honour of presenting it to me; and more especially for the favourable sentiments with which he accompanied it.

Buchan and Thomas Jefferson selected Benjamin Rush, a signatory of the Declaration of Independence, who had actively worked to eliminate an epidemic that had hit America's east coast. The Earl of Buchan in June 1791 sent this snuff box with a Scottish painter on his way to America for commissioned work (possibly to do a portrait of Jefferson), to deliver it by hand to Jefferson. The artist made it safely across the waters and took a stagecoach from New York to Mount Vernon to make the delivery. En route to Jefferson, the snuff box was stolen in a stagecoach robbery and disappeared.

In 1956, a woman donated it to the DAR, claiming that it had come into the possession of Commodore Decatur of the

United States Navy, who had given it to Catherine Clark, who passed it on to her son, Voley L. Williams, who was a pioneer settler in Illinois. It had been in his family's possession for over 100 years.

The search to verify that this is actually the box in question is still ongoing.

What a great story.

As I continued the research, poking around in files on Buchan's correspondences with Washington and others, I found a second possible version of the story:

After the executors of Washington's estate returned the box to Buchan with a copy of Washington's will, he decreed that the box be set aside:

> for the University of Washington with a Golden Pen to which there may be annually offered medals by the States to honour of such students therein as shall be found in comparative trial to have made not only the greatest progress in useful knowledge during the whole of their course of Education but shall at the same time have been found to be most exemplary in their conduct... 'most friendly to Republican Government and to the true Liberties of Mankind' in words of the great Founder himself [see Buchan's 'Observations respecting the Will of General Washington'].

Since finding this information, I have been in contact with the George Washington University, Mt Vernon historical site, and the Masonic lodge at which George Washington was an active member. I have sent the information regarding the travels of the snuff box, with a request for any and all information they may find. I have yet to hear anything, but will continue on this strange quest to discover the movements of this unusual historic artefact and its present whereabouts. Once located (if ever), I would like very much to see it returned 'on loan' to Scotland for public view.

Whichever story is true, they're both examples of the connections between Scotland and America and the theme of Freedom. This snuff box actually took the very same steps that we have traced in this journey of democracy and freedom. Starting with William Wallace as a young man sleeping in an oak tree in Scotland, and later hiding from his English foes in this same tree after a great defeat in battle; this snuff box's wood being cut from that same oak and being presented as a gift to a well-known man in Scotland; this same man, the 11th Earl of Buchan, in turn gifting this snuff box to the recently-elected president of a newly-formed country, which had fought the same foe and won its freedom many years later.

Now we come full circle, with a race of men moved to fight for independence and secure for their own the right to live in freedom, with their 'natural rights' intact. From Scotland in the 13th century through the Rising of the Jacobites in the 18th, to America and the Revolution there, and now back to Scotland, with its own parliament in operation once again.

And it continues on:

16 January 2007 marked 300 years since the Act of Union, and the people of Scotland are once again talking about complete independence from Britain. They may soon have it, through a vote cast by the people.

Good luck to you, and to all Scots, and the everlasting ideals of the 'Rights of Man' and Freedom – wherever in the world you may be living now.

AFTERWORD ON DEMOCRACY

IN THIS MODERN WORLD, the word 'democracy' is tossed around like a ball by the media, politicians, and heads of state. Webster's Dictionary defines democracy as 'a government in which the people hold the ruling power either directly or through elected representatives; rule by the ruled'. By this definition, modern states that have chosen democratic rule should be run according to the needs and wishes of all those within their boundaries. But I fear that is not the case. Something has been lost along the way, and the power of such nations has been placed almost completely in the hands of the few that represent them.

This disjointed approach, where the 'people's voice' is not vocalised, and the majority is no longer actively involved, leads to the slow and painful breakdown of the system of democracy itself.

The public must be ever watchful of those they have placed in positions of decision-making. They must not simply make their choice by a cast vote and hope that all will work out for the best. Somehow we've come to believe that our power lies in the vote alone, like ordering a meal, where someone else will do the cooking and serving of it; the job of cleaning up afterwards will always ultimately fall back on the people.

An elected official is placed in a position to work for the people. If you hired someone to work for you, there would be at the least a period of training and intervals of monitoring. You wouldn't just leave them to figure it out on their own, and let them guess what your needs and expectations might be. They would be taught what the objectives, approaches and end-goals of the operation were and how to achieve them. The people are the 'managers' and 'owners' of the democratic nation. And a great responsibility comes along with that ownership.

When you elect someone to oversee your city, county, or country, it is like handing them your wallet, the keys to your home and car, and access to your bank accounts, because you are handing them the power to affect each of these things in your personal life. If you gave this power to anyone else, you would, no doubt, keep a close eye on them, watching their spending patterns, making sure your needs were being provided for, and that your standard of living was not changing for anything but the better.

Democracy can't be shoved down the throats of those who are unwilling, but must first be embraced by the body of people, then sought out and hopefully achieved. The people have to sacrifice themselves to democracy and the ideals of it. This sacrifice embodies the need for tolerance of others and their rights in society. Democracy, once found, has to be constantly cultivated, fed, watered and weeded for any hope of growth and harvest. One nation cannot make another become democratic; this can only be achieved from within.

Human nature is such that we tend to learn more from our defeats than we do our victories. Victory can often bring an arrogance with it, where a simple feeling of accomplishment would do. A shift can occur, where the once 'conquered' become the 'conquerors'. The fight for one's freedoms can unleash an unbridled feeling of knowing what's right for everyone. Sometimes the 'oppressed', once finding their victory over the 'oppressors', become the new oppressors of other peoples in other lands. We can take to monitoring others, in society, and in the world, instead of keeping a mindful eye on those that have been entrusted with the power in our own backyard.

Democracy cannot be held for long by any nation if the people overseeing it become complacent about the rights once hard-fought for, and take them for granted, as a birthright.

Democracy is a privilege, delivered to the people, and must be nurtured.

Democracy is contained within the ideals surrounding the basic 'rights of man', not the rights of a governing body or the lawful mandates it has set in place. These things are in place to support and uphold the rights of the people within the nation, not to bend, sway, and strip these rights away, under the guise of doing 'what is right for the nation' or 'what is right for the world at large'.

A dangerous shift can take place where the rights and needs of the people suddenly give way to the needs of the nation as a whole. Programmes to support the people are replaced by programmes to 'protect' the nation. Monies set in place originally to assist the people, so they can remain strong, educated, healthy, and progressive, start to shift into programmes that aim to strengthen the nation itself. A crust of protection forms on the outside of the nation, giving the appearance of strength, while the contents within decay through lack of support. The people become weakened, their energies are spent on surviving, and society starts to break down. The people become disconnected from the power they once held, their voice becomes a whisper easily ignored (if heard at all), and those placed in office, originally to aid the people, start to believe that they hold all the power. And sadly... they do.

The strength of a nation is in its people, and it is the people who have the responsibility to uphold its basic tenets. But first they have to understand what these tenets are, and what the responsibility of each citizen is to keep these things in operation, even though centuries may have passed since this was all set down for them.

And we must understand the sacrifice of those that came before us, to ensure these rights for us, and likewise be willing to contribute our own sacrifice, diligence and hard work to retain and sustain these rights, now and for the generations to come.

And always remember...

It's great that you're proud of your ancestors.

But the question at hand is...
are your ancestors proud of you?

And what have you done for your country lately,
with no want of your own?

LINDA MACDONALD-LEWIS
MAY 2009

CHRONOLOGY OF EVENTS

BACKGROUND

*c.*600s BC — Solon lays the foundation of ideals that allows Cleisthenes to usher in radical reform, resulting in Athens' democratic constitution 100 years later.

*c.*100s AD — Roman conquest of Britain begins.

*c.*200s — Hadrian's Wall is built, marking the northern-most reaches of the Roman Empire.

*c.*500s — Roman forces withdraw from Britian.
St Columba arrives on Iona, off the coast of Scotland, and founds a monastery.
St Patrick arrives in Ireland, bringing Christianity to the Celtic tribes.

*c.*600s — St Augustine is sent to England and becomes the first Archbishop of Canterbury.

*c.*790s — Vikings pillage Iona.

840s — Kenneth MacAlpine brings the Picts and the Scots under one rule.

1215 — The Magna Carta Libertatum (Great Charter of Freedoms) is issued in England.

PART ONE

1249 — Alexander III takes the throne of Scotland at the age of eight, upon the death of his father.

1251 — Alexander III marries Margaret.

1263 — October, Battle of Largs – Scots defeat Viking invaders on the west coast of Scotland; reputed to be where William Wallace's father and brother died.
King Haakon of Norway (whose landholds include Orkney and Shetland) dies at midnight of 15/16 December.

1266 — Treaty between the Scots and the Norse.

1274 — Robert the Bruce is born at Turnberry Castle.

1275 — Queen Margaret dies, leaving one child, also named Margaret.

1281 — Alexander III's daughter Margaret marries Eric II of Norway.

1283 — Margaret (Eric II's wife and queen) dies while giving birth to their daughter, also named Margaret (known as the 'Maid of Norway').

1285	Alexander III marries Yolande of Dureux.
1286	18 March, Alexander III dies.
1290	Treaty of Birgham.
	The Maid of Norway dies in Orkney, en route to Scotland.
1292	30 November, John Balliol is crowned King of Scotland.
1295	An agreement between Scotland and France is made – the beginning of the 'Auld Alliance'.
1296	30 March, massacre at Berwick-upon-Tweed by Edward I and his army.
	27 April, battle at Dunbar. Edward I plunders Scotland and removes many of her treasures, including the Stone of Destiny.
	8 July, John Balliol is captured by Edward I, and stripped of his mantle as King of Scotland.
	The Ragman Rolls is signed and sealed.
1297	William Wallace appears in history, killing the Sheriff of Lanark in May.
	The Battle of Loudon Hill and the Battle at Scone.
	By July, the nobles of Scotland accept terms with the English at Irvine.
	August, Wallace joins up with Andrew Moray at Stirling and prepare for battle.
	11 September, victory for the Scots at the Battle of Stirling Bridge.
	Wallace and Moray are made joint 'Guardians of Scotland'.
	November, Moray dies from wounds received at the Battle of Stirling Bridge, leaving Wallace as sole Guardian of Scotland.
1298	22 July, Battle of Falkirk. The Scots are defeated by Edward's army, but Wallace escapes.
	Wallace steps down from being Guardian. Bruce and John Comyn are made Guardians.
1299	Wallace leaves the country.
	William Lamberton is made third Guardian.
1300	Bruce resigns from being Guardian and is replaced by Sir Gilbert, First Lord of Umfraville.
1302	Edward I makes a nine-month truce with Scotland.
1303	Edward I begins his invasion of Scotland once again.

1304   John (the Red) Comyn negotiates a surrender to Edward I. All Scottish leaders sign, except Wallace.

Bruce and Lamberton make a secret pact of alliance.

1305   3 August, Wallace is captured at Robroyston and taken to London.

22 August, Wallace arrives in London and is imprisoned.

23 August, the trial and execution of Wallace at Smithfield, in London.

1306   10 February, Bruce kills Comyn at Greyfriar's Monastery, Dumfries.

25 March, Bruce is crowned Robert I, King of Scots.

Bruce is excommunicated by the Pope.

1307   In the spring, Edward I marches through Scotland, dispersing the Bruce's lands and proclaiming his excommunication by the church.

Bruce's family and friends are captured by the English. Some are executed, others imprisoned.

7 July, Edward I dies en route to Scotland.

Edward II takes the throne.

1309   March, King Robert holds his first parliament at St Andrews.

1310   Bruce is recognized as king by the clergy of Scotland.

Edward II gives permission for his outpost to negotiate truce with King Robert.

1313   Edward Bruce (the king's brother) puts Stirling Castle under siege, requiring relief from the English king's men by midsummer 1314.

1314   23, 24 June, the Battle of Bannockburn, a great victory for the Scots.

6 November, King Robert's parliament at Cambuskenneth.

1317   The Pope sends cardinals to England, to speak with Edward II about Scotland.

1320   6 April, the Declaration of Arbroath is sent to the Pope.

The De Soules Conspiracy. The traitors are sentenced, and their lands and holdings are dispersed among those loyal to the king.

1328   17 March, Treaty of Edinburgh (with the English) at Holyrood.

1329   7 June, death of Good King Robert the Bruce.

PART TWO

1349–50	The Black Death.
1378–82	John Wycliffe translates the Bible into the English language.
1378–1417	The Great Schism – rival popes in Rome, Italy and Avignon, France fight for control of the Roman Catholic Church.
1455	Invention of the printing process, Gutenburg completes the first printed Bible.
1492	Chrisopher Columbus 'discovers' the Americas, leading to European expansion into the American continent.
1493	Forfeiture of the Lordship of the Isles by the Clan Donald (MacDonalds).
1509	Henry VIII comes to the English throne.
1517	Martin Luther speaks out against the doctrines of the Catholic Church. The Reformation takes hold.
1541	John Knox leads the Reformation in Scotland.
1547	Henry VIII dies.
1603	James VI and I takes the throne, uniting the crowns of Scotland and England for the first time in history, on the death of Elizabeth I.
1625	Charles I comes to the throne.
1649	Charles I is executed, and Oliver Cromwell rules the new 'Commonwealth'.
1660	Charles II reclaims the throne.
1689	4 April, James VII and II (Catholic) is dethroned and forfeits the crowns of both Scotland and England. William of Orange and Mary (Protestants) take the throne. James VII and II, his family, and his court flee into exile. 27 July, Battle of Killiecrankie, led by 'Bonnie Dundee'; the first Jacobite act of defiance.
1692	13 February, Massacre of Glencoe.
1694	Mary dies, leaving William to rule alone.
1695	Act of Parliament to create the Darien Scheme.
1702	William of Orange dies and Anne (Mary's sister) takes the crown.
1707	The Union of the Parliaments.
1708	James Stuart (the Old Pretender) tries and fails to reclaim his throne.
1714	Anne dies and the first George from the House of Hanover comes to the throne.

1715	6 September, the Jacobites raise the standard of their 'rightful king' at Braemar, gathering support for a rebellion.
	Battle of Sheriffmuir.
1719	10 June, Battle of Glenshiel.
	James Stuart marries Clementina Sobieski.
1720	Bonnie Prince Charlie (the Young Pretender) is born Charles Edward Stuart.
1722	Flora MacDonald is born.
1743	Cardinal de Tencin is appointed Prime Minister of France by Louis XV.
1744	29 January, Bonnie Prince Charlie arrives in Paris.
1745	The Year of the Prince and the Jacobite Rising of the '45.
1746	The Battle of Culloden, with drastic results.
	Flora MacDonald helps the Prince escape out of Scotland.
1747	The Proscription Act is passed.
1760–1775	40,000 Scots leave for North America.
1775	100,000 Ulster Scots migrate to the North American colonies.
1782	The Proscription Act is repealed.

PART THREE

1760	George III of the House of Hanover takes the crown of England.
1764	The English parliament passes legislative Acts restricting the North American colonists' trade and other activities.
	The Sons of Liberty are formed and a 'Declaration of Grievances' is sent to the English leaders.
	The phrase 'Taxation without Representation' becomes a popular slogan of the Revolutionaries.
1766	The Stamp Act.
1767	The Townshend Act.
1768	The Massachusetts legislative body is dissolved by the British.
1769	Virginia's governing body is dissolved by the British.
1770	The Townshend Act is reduced by the British.
	5 March, the Boston Massacre.
1772	*The Gaspee*, a customs schooner, is attacked.
	Samuel Adams calls for a Committee of Correspondences.

1773	The Tea Act reduces taxes on British imported tea.
	The Boston Tea Party.
1774	The Coercive Acts, the Port Bill and the Massachusetts Government Act are enacted.
	Colonists organise further and name delegates for the first Continental Congress.
	The British seize ammunitions from Massachusetts.
	Militiamen rise up by the thousands from the colonies.
	The Minute Men are formed for quick military action.
1775	New England Restraining Acts.
	Committee of Safety.
	19 April, the Minute Men meet British troops at Lexington.
	The 'shot heard round the world' is fired, officially starting the American War of Independence.
	Paul Revere makes his 'midnight ride' to warn of incoming British troops at Concord.
	10 May, the Continental Congress meets again. George Washington is named Commander-in-Chief.
	12 June, the Battle of Bunker Hill.
	The 'Olive Branch Petition' is sent to the British leadership.
1776	January, 'Common Sense' by Thomas Paine is released to the public.
	The 'Committee of Five' are selected to write up a document reflecting the ideals of Paine's writings.
	July, the 'Lee Resolution'.
	4 July, the Declaration of Independence is sent to the printer Dunlap.
	5 July, the Declaration of Independence is distributed to the public and to colony leaders.
	6 July, Benjamin Townes releases the Declaration of Independence on the front page of his newspaper.
	August, most of the delegates have signed the Declaration, and an engrossed copy is made.
1777–8	Winter, Washington at Valley Forge
1783	3 September, the Treaty of Paris is signed, officially ending the Revolutionary War.
1784	14 January, the Treaty is ratified by the Continental Congress.
	9 April, the Treaty is ratified by the British.
	12 May, copies of the Treaty (signed and ratified) are exchanged by the two nations.

MODERN HISTORY

1997	11 September, a referendum calling for a parliament with devolved powers in Scotland is passed. This is Scotland's first parliament since the Act of Union in 1707. (This date also marked the 700th anniversay of the Battle of Stirling Bridge.)
1998	The USA and Canada pass legislation marking 6 April as National Tartan Day.
	The Scotland Act establishes the new government as the Scottish Executive.
1999	6 May, a general election is held to establish the members of the Scottish Parliament.
	12 May, Dr Winnie Ewing declares, 'the Scottish parliament, which adjourned on 25 March 1707, is hereby reconvened.'
	1 July, power transfers from Westminster to the Scottish Parliament.
2004	The new Scottish Parliament building opens, designed by architect Enric Miralles.
2007	January, 300th Anniversary of the Act of Union.
	3 May, the Scottish National Party (SNP) wins the general election in Scotland, with Alex Salmond becoming Scotland's First Minister.
	2 September, the SNP rebrands the Scottish Executive as the Scottish Government.

SELECT BIBLIOGRAPHY

The Declaration of Abroath, edited by James Adam (Herald Press, Abroath, 1993, 1995).

The Bruce, John Barbour (1375; republished Glasgow, W. MacLellan 1964).

Scots in the USA, Jenni Calder (Luath Press, Edinburgh, 2006).

The Declaration of Arbroath: For Freedom Alone, Edward J. Cowan (Tuckwell Press, East Lothian, Scotland).

William Wallace, Andrew Fisher (1986; reprinted John Donald Publishers, Edinburgh, 1997).

How Scots Invented the Modern World, Arthur Herman (Three Rivers Press, New York, 2001).

Glencoe and the Indians, James Hunter (Mainstream, Edinburgh 1997).

Collins Encylopaedia of Scotland, edited by John Keay and Julia Keay (Collins, London, 1994).

Blind Harry's Wallace, William Hamilton of Gilbertfield, edited by Elspeth King (Luath Press, Edinburgh, 1998).

Slaughter Under Trust: Glencoe 1692, Donald J Macdonald (Delaware Free Press, 1982).

Clan Donald, Donald J. Macdonald of Castleton (MacDonald Publishers, Loanhead, Midlothian, 1978).

Prince Charlie and His Ladies, Compton Mackenzie (Alfred A. Knopp, New York, 1935).

The Scottish Chiefs, Jane Porter (Thomas Y. Crowell, New York, revised 1841).

On the Trail of Robert the Bruce, David R. Ross (Luath Press, Edinburgh, 1999).

On the Trail of William Wallace, David R. Ross (Luath Press, Edinburgh, 1999).

On the Trail of Bonnie Prince Charlie, David R. Ross (Luath Press, Edinburgh, 2000).

For Freedom: The Last Days of William Wallace, David R. Ross (Luath Press, Edinburgh, 2006).

Bannockburn, Peter Reese (Canongate, Edinburgh, 2000).

Reportage Scotland: History in the Making, Louise Yeoman (Luath Press, Edinburgh, 2000).

James the Good: The Black Douglas, David R. Ross (Luath Press, Edinburgh, 2008).

INDEX

Some other books published by **LUATH** PRESS

Scots in the USA

Jenni Calder
ISBN 1 905222 06 8 PBK £8.99

The map of the United States is peppered with Scottish place-names and America's telephone directories are filled with surnames illustrating Scottish ancestry. Increasingly, Americans of Scottish extraction are visiting Scotland in search of their family history. All over Scotland and the United States there are clues to the Scottish-American relationship, the legacy of centuries of trade and communication as well as that of departure and heritage.

The experiences of Scottish settlers in the United States varied enormously, as did their attitudes to the lifestyles that they left behind and those that they began anew once they arrived in North America.

Scots in the USA discusses why they left Scotland, where they went once they reached the United States, and what they did when they got there.

A reminder of the days when Scots were inventors, entrepreneurs and pioneers, by the time you turn the last page, if you're not Scottish you'll want to be.
THE DAILY RECORD

Scots in Canada

Jenni Calder
ISBN 1 84282 038 9 PBK £7.99

The story of the Scots who went to Canada, from the 17th century onwards.

In Canada there are nearly as many descendants of Scots as there are people living in Scotland; almost five million Canadians ticked the 'Scottish origin' box in the most recent Canadian Census. Many Scottish families have friends or relatives in Canada.

Thousands of Scots were forced from their homeland, while others chose to leave, seeking a better life. As individuals, families and communities, they braved the wild Atlantic Ocean, many crossing in cramped under-rationed ships, unprepared for the fierce Canadian winter. And yet Scots went on to lay railroads, found banks and exploit the fur trade, and helped form the political infrastructure of modern day Canada.

... meticulously researched and fluently written.
SCOTLAND ON SUNDAY

Calder celebrates the ties that still bind Canada and Scotland in camaraderie after nearly 400 years of relations.
THE CHRONICLE HERALD,
NOVA SCOTIA

A Passion for Scotland
David R. Ross
ISBN 1 84282 019 2 PBK £5.99

This is not a history book. But it covers history.

This is not a travel guide. But some places mentioned might be worth a visit.

This is not a political manifesto. But a personal one.

Read this book. It might make you angry. It might give you hope. You might shed a tear. You might not agree with David R. Ross.

But read this book. You might rediscover your roots, your passion for Scotland.

David R. Ross is passionate about Scotland's past, and its future. In this heartfelt journey through Scotland's story, he shares his passion for what it means to be a Scot, tackling the Act of Union, the Jacobite rebellion and revealing, for the first time, the final resting places of all Scotland's Kings and Queens.

A Passion for Scotland *sounds a clarion call to Scots worldwide to revive genuine patriotism.*
SCOTTISH TOURIST GUIDE

Wallace Muse: poems inspired by the life & legacy of William Wallace
Edited by Lesley Duncan/Elspeth King
ISBN 1 905222 29 7 PBK £8.99

Sir William Wallace – bloodthirsty and battle-hardened hero, liberator and creator of Scotland. Wallace the man was a complex character – loved by the Scots, loathed by the English, a terror to some, an inspirational leader to others. No matter what side you are on, William Wallace is an unmistakable and unforgettable historical figure whose actions at the Battle of Stirling Bridge helped free the Scottish nation. The life and legend of Wallace has been a Muse providing inspiration to poets and artists from Scotland and across the globe for 700 years. From great epic to McGonagall, the violent to the poignant, this collection highlights the impact that the memory of Wallace has made on the nation's culture for centuries.

Luath Press Limited
committed to publishing well written books worth reading

LUATH PRESS takes its name from Robert Burns, whose little collie Luath (*Gael.*, swift or nimble) tripped up Jean Armour at a wedding and gave him the chance to speak to the woman who was to be his wife and the abiding love of his life. Burns called one of 'The Twa Dogs' Luath after Cuchullin's hunting dog in Ossian's *Fingal*. Luath Press was established in 1981 in the heart of Burns country, and is now based a few steps up the road from Burns' first lodgings on Edinburgh's Royal Mile.

Luath offers you distinctive writing with a hint of unexpected pleasures.

Most bookshops in the UK, the US, Canada, Australia, New Zealand and parts of Europe either carry our books in stock or can order them for you. To order direct from us, please send a £sterling cheque, postal order, international money order or your credit card details (number, address of cardholder and expiry date) to us at the address below. Please add post and packing as follows: UK – £1.00 per delivery address; overseas surface mail – £2.50 per delivery address; overseas airmail – £3.50 for the first book to each delivery address, plus £1.00 for each additional book by airmail to the same address. If your order is a gift, we will happily enclose your card or message at no extra charge.

Luath Press Limited
543/2 Castlehill
The Royal Mile
Edinburgh EH1 2ND
Scotland

Telephone: 0131 225 4326 (24 hours)
Fax: 0131 225 4324
email: sales@luath.co.uk
Website: www.luath.co.uk